OLD LADY KILLERS

Ronald E Bowers

Former Senior Prosecutor

Los Angeles County District Attorney's Office

Some names and locations have been changed to protect the privacy of individuals connected with these cases. Certain events and statements have been inferred from the facts of these cases as well as from public articles about these cases.

Ronald E. Bowers, Publisher
losangelestruecrime@aol.com

ISBN 978-1-7325281-4-7

First release March 2015

Second release June 2017

INTRODUCTION

One day I was deeply immersed in preparing homicide cases for trial, when one of my paralegal stopped by my open door and announced that the Major Crimes Division had just been assigned the 'Old Ladies' case. I didn't want to show my ignorance; however, I couldn't place what case she was talking about. I responded with the comment, "Which Old Ladies case are you talking about?" She said, "You know, the two old gals who ran over those homeless men for the life insurance."

I had a vague recollection of the case from hearing about it in the news media. I asked how old were the women and was told they were in the septuagenarian range. The paralegal recited the facts to me, relating how despicable the actions of the women were, and in no uncertain language said, "These two old broads truly deserve the Death Penalty for all the years of Premeditation to kill the most helpless and vulnerable in society." That remark aroused my curiosity as to how any prosecutor could get 12 jurors to agree on the Death Penalty in a case involving two little old ladies.

My knowledge about the Death Penalty law dates back to when I tried such cases under the old statute. After the Death Penalty was declared void by the California Supreme Court in 1974, I was one of the very first attorneys who tried a case under the new Death Penalty law. So much of the so-called New Death Penalty law had been left vague, and we had to speculate as to the proper way to litigate such cases. In order to create new procedures for such cases, I, and a group of senior prosecutors, created a new Death Penalty Manual to spell out the proper procedure for the new Death Penalty cases. (The author realizes most readers have strong beliefs regarding the Death Penalty. This book doesn't take a position either for or against the Death Penalty, since it is an issue to be decided by the public in each state.)

For years I had handled Death Penalty cases, and I found the most challenging part for me was deciding whether the DA's Office should seek the Death Penalty in a particular case. The DA's Office had developed a criterion which listed 12 issues to consider in deciding whether to seek the Death Penalty. Yet that procedure didn't work well as to the two cases we will be discussing in this book. The first case to be reviewed involved two little old ladies who obtained dozens of life insurance policies for homeless men just to kill them so they could collect millions of dollars from those policies.

My experience has been that it is extremely difficult to obtain the Death Penalty on cases involving **female defendants**. Then, when you add the fact that the women are in their **70s**, your chances of obtaining the Death Penalty are remote to none. Simply put, no one wants to impose the Death Penalty on someone who projects the appearance of their grandmother.

The Sante Kimes case involved a woman who was in her 70s when she and her son went on a crime wave across the country. Although Sante Kimes didn't commit the murders herself, she instructed her son to carry them out at her request. What distinguishes this case was the fact that the defendant, Sante Kimes, had been convicted of the murder of a notable woman in New York. By the time Sante arrived in Los Angeles, she had already received a life term in prison. Sante Kimes had been tangled up in crimes or scams all her life. She had an extensive criminal record, just the opposite of the two little old ladies who were mainly involved in insurance fraud and filing bogus lawsuits against large companies.

There were many people in the DA's Office who believed that Sante Kimes, Helen Golay, and Olga Rutterschmidt all deserved the Death Penalty. But of the three, Sante Kimes was the most serious contender for the Death Penalty.

I have been involved in the writing of numerous True Crime books and my objective is to provide you, the reader, with the facts. Jack Webb as Sgt. Joe Friday in his ***Dragnet*** TV series used the expression, "Just the facts, Ma'am." That concept works well when you know all the facts; however, many times only some of the facts are actually known. That is what occurred in both these cases. No one was privy to all the facts, and that was the challenge in trying to write about these cases. Luckily for me, I was in the right place at the right times so I gained incredible insight on both of these cases.

My association with the Golay and Rutterschmidt case occurred in a strange way. The prosecutor who had been assigned this case was embroiled in several major cases. The plan was that she would organize and prepare the Old Ladies case. When it was clear she wouldn't be available, I was asked to take a look at the case and create a PowerPoint presentation for the administration to review in order to decide whether to proceed with the Death Penalty allegation. That was when I had to become a quick learner of all the facts about the case. Det. Dennis Kilcoyne from LAPD Robbery Homicide Division was the lead investigator who answered the millions of questions I had about the case.

What I gleaned from the facts of the case was that this was more than a homicide case. It was a combined murder case with all the elements of a major fraud case. For a prosecutor, a major fraud case is particularly challenging to explain to jurors since it involves hundreds of documents. Those types of cases are tedious and tend to be boring for the jurors. Most jurors become lost in the minutiae and lose focus of what is relevant, such as crucial dates, amounts, and companies involved.

I asked Det. Kilcoyne for copies of all the life insurance policies. From each policy, I distilled the pertinent data on a chart to determine the best way to display it. The idea was to streamline the information so the jurors could concentrate on only what they needed to know. The old expression from the Watergate Scandal era—"Follow the Money"—could readily apply in this case. It was vital that the jury see how Helen Golay was the person who was behind supplying all the money for the payment of the life insurance premiums.

Other facts I wanted to convey to the jurors were the contribution made by each of the women. I used one slide to illustrate Helen Golay's role as the mastermind of the scheme. It showed her aptitude in keeping track of all the life insurance policies, especially the key dates to pay the insurance premium. On another slide I displayed a photo of Olga Rutterschmidt and listed her role, which included providing 'Room and Board' for the homeless men. Her job was to maintain contact with these men over the years.

For over six months I worked with the detectives and prosecutors to hone a PowerPoint presentation to explain what happened and who was involved. As a result, I became deeply immersed in the facts and evidence in this bizarre case. Over my 43 years of prosecuting crooks, I have never seen two elderly ladies so cold and calculating. They tell a story about human nature that few people have a chance to experience. I knew someday after I retired that I would attempt to tell their story.

The Sante Kimes case lingered for years before the trial commenced. She and her son were implicated in murdering David Kazdin on March 14, 1998. Shortly after this murder they went on a wild nation-wide crime spree, commencing on the Pacific

Coast and finally terminating on the Atlantic Coast. When they reached New York, this notorious mother-son team were eventually arrested. Since California had the Death Penalty and New York did not, it was presumed that the arrestees would be immediately transferred to California so they could be first tried in the case involving the David Kazdin murder. If they were convicted and received the Death Penalty, then it would not be necessary to prosecute them in New York.

The Los Angeles District Attorney's Office immediately brought me in to organize the trial that was expected. However, the Kimeses didn't waive extradition and both of them were tried in New York for the murder of Irene Silverman and various other fraud charges. Ultimately, both of them were convicted in NY of first-degree murder and received a sentence of 120 years to life in prison. As a result, it took years before they were extradited to California. My knowledge of the case was over a long period of time and the issues kept fluctuating.

The DA's Office was caught between a rock and a hard place when we were faced with both Sante Kimes and Kenny Kimes arriving on our doorstep. Both murder cases were different. As to Sante's case, we only had circumstantial evidence of her involvement. But as to Kenny, we had direct evidence against him, if his crime partner, Shane Lane, testified to being with Kenny when he did the shooting.

Some people in the media thought it was a waste of time to prosecute the two of them in California. But the LA DA's Office believed that both of the Kimeses should be held accountable for their crimes. This mother-son crime team had an incredible bond that bound them together to commit such horrific crimes. The media labeled them the new Bonny and Clyde. They were looked upon as a two-headed monster joined at the hip. So, it was like a bolt of lightning coming out of the sky when Kenny's Public Defender came forth with an incredible offer. Kenny would be **willing**

to testify against his mother if the DA would allow him to plead guilty to murder and receive only a life sentence in the Kazdin murder.

As close as Kenny had always been to his mother, Sante, it was not surprising that he would turn against her to save himself from being executed. One wondered, what type of ungrateful son had Sante Kimes raised? This was a tough decision for the DA's Office since it was like negotiating with the devil himself. All the DA had to do was agree not to pursue the Death Penalty on Kenny for his willingness to testify against his mother. Initially, it was wondered whether any juror would give any credence to Kenny's testimony, since he was the one who actually pulled the trigger in the Kazdin murder. It was hard to decide who was the most culpable between Sante and Kenny. It was clear that Sante called the shots but it was Kenny who did the actual killing and disposing of the body.

Being a prosecutor is an unusual job. One minute you try to seek justice by removing criminals from the streets, and in the same breathe, you are making deals with the 'scum of the earth' in order to try to catch a bigger fish. There are office policies as to when and how to grant favorable treatment in co-defendant cases. It is easy to say that you don't want to deal with criminal-minded people, but sometimes it is necessary to in order to remove the truly horrific killers from society by placing them in prison.

Fortunately, I didn't have to make the final decision of granting leniency to Kenny, but I was stuck trying to put the case together by using his testimony. At times, you almost wanted to take a shower after dealing with such despicable individuals like Kenny, since you don't want to breathe the same air he exhaled. But I have to admit the evidence he provided us was crucial in nailing his mother for all of her evil ways.

Since I was the one who initially worked on the preparation of the case, I had to read and discuss the case with the detectives. For over a year I became personally familiar with the facts of this case. What I have done for you, the reader, is take the best information I learned throughout all the investigation and trials and then write this story. Obviously, I am not privy to the exact words spoken between Helen Golay and Olga Rutterschmidt or in the case of Sante Kimes and Kenny Kimes, but I have inferred what in all probability was said and done.

I apologize to the purists True Crime readers who only want the exact words that were spoken by the suspects as contained in transcripts. The problem with these two cases is that we will never know for sure who did what, since in the Golay and Rutterschmidt case neither of the women testified or ever gave a statement to the police as to each of their roles in the killings. In the Kimeses case, both mother and son tell different versions of the facts. In my experience as a prosecutor, I never saw such human beings who were more malicious and premeditated than this group. So please sit back in your favorite comfortable chair and enjoy what is my best interpretation of the facts from all that I have learned about both cases. You will forever change your mindset about the grandmotherly types as being sweet and innocent. You may come to realize that granny can be one of the Old Lady Killers.

CONTENTS

CHAPTER 1 Going Out To Dinner....1
CHAPTER 2 Picking up a Guest....9
CHAPTER 3 The Last Supper....15
CHAPTER 4 Cruising the Sunset Strip....19
CHAPTER 5 Looking for a Dark Alley....23
CHAPTER 6 Accidents Do Happen....29
CHAPTER 7 Need a Tow....35
CHAPTER 8 Who Is Helen Golay?....43
CHAPTER 9 Who Is Olga Rutterschmidt?....47
CHAPTER10 Hit-and-Run Investigation....51
CHAPTER 11 Connecting the Two Cases....55
CHAPTER 12 Surveillance....61
CHAPTER 13 Police Have a Dilemma....65
CHAPTER 14 Arrest & Search Warrant....69
CHAPTER 15 Continuing Investigation....71
CHAPTER 16 The Story of the Sable....73
CHAPTER 17 Forensics....81
CHAPTER 18 Arranging the Insurance Policies....85
CHAPTER 19 Building a Case....91
CHAPTER 20 Ladies Talking....99
CHAPTER 21 DA's Office Preparing the Case....105
CHAPTER 22 Ready for Trial....115
CHAPTER 23 Trial....117
CHAPTER 24 Incredible Defense....125
CHAPTER 25 How It All Ended....129
CHAPTER 26 What Have We Learned?....135
CHAPTER 27 Epilogue....137
CHAPTER 28 Another Wicked Woman....141
CHAPTER 29 The Team of Kenneth Sr. and Sante....147
CHAPTER 30 Sante Takes Over....155
CHAPTER 31 Good Day for a Murder....161
CHAPTER 32 Mother-Son Team....169
CHAPTER 33 Grifters on the Move....175
CHAPTER 34 Who Was Irene Silverman?....179
CHAPTER 35 Kenny Gets Foot in The Door....183
CHAPTER 36 Death of Irene Silverman....189
CHAPTER 37 Disposing of the Body....195
CHAPTER 38 Long Afternoon....197

CHAPTER 39 Arrest And Search 199
CHAPTER 40 Ready for New York Trial 203
CHAPTER 41 Strange Defense 209
CHAPTER 42 From New York To California 219
CHAPTER 43 Sante's Trial in Los Angeles 225
CHAPTER 44 Other Prosecution Witnesses 229
CHAPTER 45 Interesting Defense 235
CHAPTER 46 Similarities between Old Ladies 243
CHAPTER 47 Epilogue 251

CHAPTER 1 GOING OUT TO DINNER

On Saturday, June 21, 2005, the summer solstice occurred at 06:46 p.m., when the sun was farthest north of the equator in the northern hemisphere. What we do know is that Helen Golay, (better known as Black Widow #1) had agreed to meet Olga Rutterschmidt (better known as Black Widow #2) since it appeared to be the perfect day to commit a highly anticipated premeditated murder. Helen told Olga that their investment in Kenneth McDavid was becoming too expensive since he was costing them several thousand dollars each month. Some described her job as fattening up the turkeys for Christmas. Helen wasn't so crass; she merely thought it was a way of making money even though it meant that a homeless man had to be sacrificed. But to her these homeless men were going to die anyway so she gave them a good sendoff by providing them a good place to live for their last few months on the earth.

She had gone through her records, which she meticulously kept, and saw at least a dozen insurance companies that had to be paid exactly on time. Helen had been the bookkeeper type starting way back in the 1950s when she worked for Douglas Aircraft, which was housed at Clover Field in

Santa Monica. She realized that to make sure their investment paid off, she had to pay all the premiums on time so the dozens of life insurance policies that she had taken out on these homeless men wouldn't lapse. The objective was to take out numerous life insurance policies on homeless men for a period of two years. After that amount of time, the insurance companies are required by law to basically pay off policies without disputing the facts of the death. Nevertheless, Helen had become carried away with one homeless man, Kenneth McDavid, and taken out way too many policies, and now the premiums each month were becoming too extravagant. Helen and her investment partner, Olga, were going to speed up the disposal procedure by inviting the victim out to dinner, or better known as the 'Last Supper.' Olga made contact with McDavid and told him that she and Helen wanted to take him out for a special dinner.

Helen arranged to pick up Olga and later McDavid around 7:00 p.m. Helen needed to prepare the 'knockout drugs' so she opened up her medicine cabinet and mixed a concoction containing Ambien and poured it into a small bottle she placed into her purse. Now she was ready to leave. She had parked the 'Killer Car' in the alley behind her house. She walked out to the alley, passed her Mercedes SUV, which was her usual means of transportation. She walked over to a Silver 1991 Mercury Sable SUV and sat down in the driver's seat. She had this car ready for several months, waiting for the right time to set in motion the 'Disposal Mission.'

She liked being seen driving around town in her Mercedes. She didn't feel as important in this less prestigious Silver Mercury Sable, but it was perfect for the 'Killer Car' so she didn't mind driving it for this fateful event. She pulled out of the alley behind her house in Santa Monica, turning left on Ocean Park Boulevard. As she descended a slight hill, she could gaze out over the Pacific Ocean. The sun was about to set and still a few sailboats were racing, attempting to return before dark to the tranquility of the harbor at Marina Del Rey.

She made a right on Ocean Boulevard, which took her along the road that overlooked the Santa Monica bluffs. She had to brake for a red signal in front of the Santa Monica pier. Over the entrance to the pier is the legendary curved sign emblazoned "SANTA MONICA—YACHT HARBOR—SPORT FISHING & BOATING—Cafes. Tourist and locals darted in front of her car as though they were in a hurry to reach the old carousel on the pier. Helen was having a pleasant senior moment as she remembered when Paul Newman and Robert Redford filmed **The Sting** in 1973 at the carousel which is at the foot of the pier.

Traffic resumed and she drove past the chic restaurants with couples relaxing at tables gazing at the inky blue of the Pacific Ocean while waiting for the soft glow of the sunset. She could recall in her younger days when she was working at Douglas Aircraft, all the Friday lunches she and her colleagues enjoyed at the various restaurants. As she approached Santa Monica Boulevard, she made a right turn and headed eastbound. This had been the last leg of the famous Route 66, which was the highway which many people from the mid-west traveled in the 1930-50s to reach their imaginary new paradise (City of the Angels).

After traveling about three miles, she came to the large intersection at Westwood Boulevard. She made a left-hand turn and proceeded several blocks to the Bristol Farms Market, where she made another left and pulled into an alley on the back side of the market. Slowly, she proceeded down this alley, which was lined with tall fences on one side and the rear to several businesses that faced Westwood Boulevard. In the daylight it looked drab and dirty.

As one slowly meanders down the alley one has to pay attention in order to maneuver around the potholes that needed filling. When traveling down the alley, your only thought is where is another street so one can exit this bumpy alley? Helen looked from side to side as she let the Sable coast down the slight decline. When she reached the end of the alley she turned left to return to Westwood Boulevard. At that point a smile lit up Helen's face as she thought to herself, 'this will do just fine.'

As she pulled back out on Westwood Boulevard, she crossed over into the left turn lane and stopped at the red signal. After waiting for the traffic to clear, she made her left turn to continue eastbound on Santa Monica Boulevard. Two blocks down the boulevard she could see the giant Latter Day Saints (Mormon) Temple on her left. It is an imposing structure that appears to stretch all the way to the sky (it is 369 feet tall).

As Helen drove by she remembered that in 1956 she took a public tour through the Temple before the building was consecrated and closed to the public. Helen couldn't miss the golden figure on top of the temple, which is a 15-foot statue of the 'Angel Moroni' who guarded the golden plates for Joseph Smith. Originally the statue faced southeast, but later leaders had the statue changed to face due east, which pointed Helen in the direction she needed to travel.

Helen was on a 'Disposal Mission,' although it wouldn't be considered a religious undertaking. Helen had the air conditioner on, but she had the windows down for some fresh air. This 1999 Mercury Sable SUV zipped along Santa Monica Boulevard passing Century City Mall (where Christy Johnson met her killer, Victor Palelogus, whose story is described in the author's book *Meet Me for Murder*). As Helen approached the large intersection of the Avenue of the Stars, she had to wait for the signal to change.

She looked to the right for a moment and her memory drifted back to when this was the back lot for 20th Century Fox studio. That was where so many of her favorite Westerns were filmed. She turned her attention to the green signal and proceeded into the City of Beverly Hills. She drove east on Santa Monica Boulevard, which is the demarcation line for this affluent city. Those living to the left side (Northside) were the homes of the Rich and Famous, and those on the right were the wannabes who hoped someday to move up to the Rich and Famous section of the city.

Helen relished driving through Beverly Hills, where she had dreamed of living but knew that it was out of her league. She glanced to the left to see Merv Griffin's Beverly Hilton Hotel, where the Golden Globe Awards ceremony is held every February. She liked mixing with the celebrities, and as she drove by Rodeo Drive she didn't dare turn off to do a little shopping. She would be too embarrassed driving a Mercury Sable down the renowned shopping street. As she passed Rodeo Drive, she took a glance at the stores where she had spent hours window shopping.

Within seconds she was passing the City Hall structure adjacent to the police department. Her head looked to the left and could see the turnoff to Elm Street (where the Menendez brothers shot and killed their parents in this author's book *Rich Kid Killers of Beverly Hills*). She shook her head thinking about the stupidity of the Menendez Brothers in going on a spending spree after shooting to death their two parents. She couldn't fathom the level of greed that the Menendez brothers exhibited. In her mind they deserved to be caught for being so gluttonous.

As she approached La Cienega Boulevard, she could see the signal had turned red. She eased to a stop and looked south on La Cienega to the next corner, where there was a closed restaurant. (This was where Susan Murphy met the killer in the author's book *Meet Me for Murder*). As the signal changed, Helen pressed down on the accelerator and continued straight down Santa Monica Boulevard to the City of West Hollywood. This small cosmopolitan town is proud to be the center for the gay and lesbian community in the Los Angeles area. The traffic slowed with so many happy couples parading the crowded sidewalks as they visited the delightful cafes.

At this point Santa Monica Boulevard widens out, with a large center divider between east and west traffic. Helen reflected on better times in the 1950s, when trolley car tracks ran down the center of the roadway. The old red streetcars would cling clang down the center tracks. This was the main route Angelinos took to get to the beautiful beaches. Helen thought what a sad day it was when the city fathers of Los Angeles County decided to scrap all the trolley lines and replaced them with congested freeways. Helen briefly became nostalgic and she questioned the wisdom of all the imprudent decisions made in the past. As she proceeded through West Hollywood, she had to complain to herself about the traffic jam that had been created with so many cars clogging Santa Monica Boulevard.

As she approached La Brea Boulevard, she made a right turn and went down about eight blocks toward the old Hancock Park area. This was where the 'Old Money' people of Los Angeles resided in their stately mansions. The houses are picture perfect and well maintained. Not even a leaf is permitted to be out of place. Helen speculated whether she would have fitted in with the Blue Bloods of Los Angeles. This exclusive area surrounds the Wilshire Country Club, where big-money members make their business deals. But before she reached the entrance to Hancock Park she made a hard right and looked for the alley that ran parallel to La Brea. She pulled into the alley, which appeared to have been long neglected, with giant potholes and trash littering both sides.

Helen pulled the Mercury Sable to a stop at the alley's entrance. She stared down the alley and tried to visualize what it looked like five years earlier when Paul Vados was run over in this very alley. It was investigated and seemed to be an unfortunate hit-and-run. Helen remembered what a big mistake they had made when they forgot to have any form of identification in the victim's clothing. Helen would be the first to admit that one must learn from one's mistakes. This time the victim would definitely have at least two forms of identification in his pockets.

As Helen contemplated her accomplishment she still felt good about her work, in that they had made over $640,000 on Paul's unfortunate death. But the next time they would make four times as much. As she looked down the alley, she could see the figure of a homeless man walking—or more accurately staggering—his way through trash. She shook her head and said to herself, "This location would no longer do as a killing site."

She backed the Sable out of the alley and returned to La Brea Boulevard and drove to the glitz and glamour of Hollywood.

CHAPTER 2 PICKING UP A GUEST

Driving up La Brea Boulevard was depressing for Helen. She could remember when there were fine furniture stores on both sides of the street. As Helen reached Sunset Boulevard, she had to stop for the signal. She could remember when the corner contained one of those wonderful drive-in restaurants of the 50s and 60s. The waitresses moved from car to car on roller skates. For some reason the hamburgers and fries tasted better when they were delivered by waitresses on wheels. She could remember how much fun it was to come to Hollywood. The old drive-in went by way of the wrecking ball in the name of progress as several fast food restaurants took its place.

Helen headed up La Brea to Hollywood Boulevard, where she made a right turn. Her heart sunk as she looked down Hollywood Boulevard. This wasn't the town she remembered. As far as the eye could see, there were little souvenir and discount stores. People besieged the sidewalk dressed up as cartoon characters, begging the tourists for money. Helen pulled in the left-hand turn lane almost in front of the Grauman's Chinese Theater (often call the Mann's theater but now officially named the TCL Chinese Theater). In its glory days, many Hollywood movie premiers were held there. This is where the movie stars placed their hand and footprints in the cement. Strangely, this old theater built before the depression has by default become the heart of Hollywood. Tourists flock to the theater with the misguided belief that movie stars congregate there.

The only time the surrounding area is inundated with Celebrities is during the night of the Academy Awards Ceremony. The Oscars are handed out next door at the Kodak Theatre (which was later named the Coby Theatre after Kodak declared bankruptcy in 2012.) Helen was thankful this wasn't time for the Academy Awards. However, since it was a Saturday evening the traffic was reduced to a snail's pace. She hated making this turn since she had to wait three times for the signal to change because the crosswalks were saturated with tourists from all over the world.

Eventually, she made her left hand turn, but she was blocked by 'lookie loo' sightseers. When it cleared, she maneuvered her way north on Sycamore Avenue. Her next challenge would be finding a place she could pull over. She couldn't understand why her good friend Olga Rutterschmidt had to live on a street behind this tourist trap. Olga had called this tired, rundown apartment her home for almost 30 years. She had a third-floor apartment, and its only claim to fame was that it was directly behind the Grauman's Theater. For Olga, this was the most exciting place to live, even though you couldn't have visitors since there were no places to park a car.

Helen was hoping that Olga would be out in front waiting for her. It always irritated Helen when Olga wasn't at the curb. Helen couldn't see Olga since she was blocked by some trash dumpsters next to the street. Helen pulled partway into a driveway and honked her horn to catch Olga's attention.

Apparently Olga didn't recognize Helen in the Sable. There was a loud honking and Olga made herself more visible and waved at Helen. Olga quickly proceeded to the car. Without any salutation or small talk, Olga's comment to Helen was that she needed to go up to Franklin Boulevard and make a right. Helen followed Olga's directions and was eastbound on Franklin Avenue. Immediately, Helen came to a stop at the entrance to the Magic Castle. Helen couldn't remember the last time she went to see a performance at the Magic Castle.

She just had a pleasant flashback as to when she had last visited the Castle as a guest and was paraded through the various rooms to watch the magicians do their magic. She made a note to herself to make contact with a Magic Castle member in order to receive an invitation to the Castle. It is a place where magicians can become members. To enjoy their skill of sleight of hand, one needs to know a magician who is a member.

Next to the Magic Castle was the hillside road that proceeded to another Hollywood landmark. Helen could see a stream of traffic winding up the road to Yamashiro Restaurant on top of the hill. Helen remembered having dinner at the restaurant with one of her husbands. It was a gorgeous setting overlooking the lights of Hollywood. Fortunately, that was one of the few landmarks of Tinseltown that hadn't been torn down. It was time for Helen to return to the business at hand as she drove down Franklin Avenue making a zig zag in the street, which Helen was able to do even with all the traffic.

Then she made a right turn to proceed south on Cherokee Avenue to1843, the apartment house where they had paid for Kenneth McDavid to live. As the two elderly ladies traveled down Cherokee Avenue, Helen saw a vacant parking space next to the curb and pulled over to stop. Helen wanted to review with Olga what they needed to do to make sure everything they had planned would go off without a hitch. Helen told Olga that she had to make certain that Kenneth had at least two forms of identification on him. Olga nodded that she had told Kenneth to bring his identification with him. Helen asked if there was anyone who would know that Kenneth was leaving with them. Olga assured Helen that Kenneth was by himself. Then Helen told Olga, "Then let's do it". This was stated without any emotion, only with the tone of a common business transaction.

Helen pulled back onto Cherokee Avenue and continued to the front of Kenneth's apartment house. Luckily the driveway was empty, so she pulled into a driveway and stopped. Olga quickly exited the car and scurried to Kenneth's apartment. She knocked on the door and eventually Kenneth McDavid opened the door. Olga said that they were going to take him to dinner. McDavid asked how long would it take. He was concerned about getting back to his apartment to see one of his favorite TV programs. He indicated that he would take his bike and he could ride home after dinner. Olga thought it would be okay and told him to bring his bike along. When they got to the car, Olga told Helen that Kenneth had a bike he wanted to bring along.

Helen agreed and said that he could place it in the back of the SUV. Kenneth leaned over and took off the front wheel so the bike would easily slide into the rear section of the Sable. He had brought along a helmet so that he would be safe just in case he was involved in a traffic accident. He placed the helmet on top of the bike and pulled down the rear door, walked around, and sat down in the back seat of the car.

The following graphic page shows the two suspects with victim McDavid. Also shown are some of the locations where they paid for housing the victim. Likewise, there is a photo of the silver Mercury Sable they drove that night that was used to kill the victim.

Graphic 1

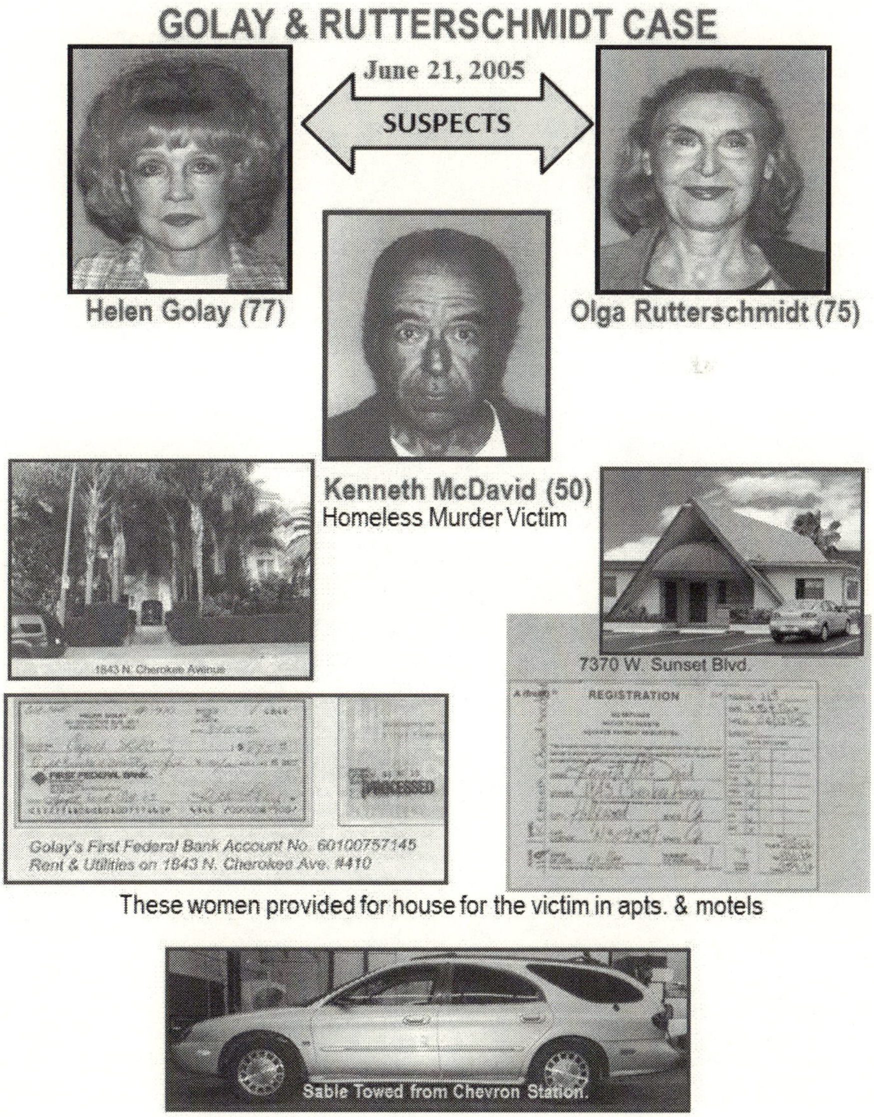

This was car they used to drive over the victim

CHAPTER 3 THE LAST SUPPER

Everyone was seated in the car, and Helen headed for the restaurant. Since Olga had been in the restaurant business in Hollywood for years, she knew which restaurants were good versus those that were merely tourist traps. They traveled several blocks east on Hollywood Boulevard to Gower Street, where they made a left turn and stopped at the corner of Carlos and Gower.

The building in front of them was the imposing Hollywood Presbyterian Church. Helen reminded Kenneth that it was where they first met him, several years earlier, when he was living in a cluster of cardboard boxes. Olga reminded him that he was now living in a nice apartment because of their generosity. The church was closed at this late hour. He was very grateful to the parishioners at this church. They had reached out and given him hope as well as a second chance in turning his life around. He couldn't thank these two women enough for all they had done to lift him out of the hell of homelessness to the pleasant lifestyle he had been enjoying. At no time did they ask him to do anything for them, except the fact they requested him to stop drinking for his own well-being.

This was a moving moment for all three of them as they sat in the Mercury Sable, better described as the 'Killer Car.' As the women turned away from the church, they were looking at ground zero for every recruit of LAPD. The women didn't realize they were parked next to the crime scene of the notorious Onion Field kidnapping. It was this exact spot that on March 9, 1963 two LAPD detectives, Ian Campbell and Karl Hettinger, made a traffic stop of a 1946 Ford driven by Gregory Powell and his pal Jimmy Lee Smith. The detectives thought those individuals looked suspicious but didn't realize they were armed robbers. The detectives split up as they approached the stopped vehicle. Detective Hettinger escorted the passenger, Smith, to the sidewalk. Detective Campbell asked the driver, Powell, to exit the vehicle. As the officer walked toward the curb, Powell pulled out a gun and stuck it in Det. Campbell's back. They walked toward the sidewalk. Detective Campbell told his partner he had a gun and to hand over his gun.

This moment in history has been a teaching moment for every police cadet class. Officer Hettinger had to make a split-second decision. Should he comply and turn over his gun, or should he resist and possibly get his partner shot? He gave up his gun and both were kidnapped and taken to an onion field near Bakersfield, California, where Detective Campbell was shot in cold blood. The other officer was able to break away and eventually escape. The kidnappers were convicted of murder. However, Officer Hettinger was made out as an errant officer who in the end got his partner killed. This officer had a nervous breakdown and had to leave police work for making the mistake. Thus, began the police tenet that **AN OFFICER SHOULD NEVER GIVE UP HIS WEAPON**.

Little did Helen or Olga know they were on the most hallowed ground for LAPD officers. Helen continued to make various turns until she reached a strip mall that included a restaurant with a large parking lot. Olga told Helen this was the right restaurant, although she didn't say out loud that this was the place for Kenneth's 'Last Supper.' They parked the car and entered the restaurant and asked for a table in the back where it was quieter and darker. Kenneth was kind of excited that he was being treated to dinner. They told him he could have anything on the menu.

Since they were trying to make it a special occasion, they agreed to have drinks. For months, Olga had been preventing Kenneth from having any money for alcohol. So Kenneth was pleased that alcohol was going to be permitted. Consumption of alcohol had been the bane of his existence. Nonetheless, he was in the company of these two elderly benefactors and he couldn't be in safer company. They all ordered. The drinks came first and he was delighted to be able to consume alcohol without feeling guilty. Before their main dishes came, they ordered another round of drinks. He was beginning to unwind and felt thoroughly relaxed. How fortunate for him to have met these two generous ladies who took such a special interest in him.

He couldn't remember his family providing such attention to him. His family had written him off and had abandoned him to live the dirty life as a homeless drifter. These ladies, out of the goodness of their hearts, had gotten him off the streets, and now he had a roomy apartment to call home. What was so nice about these women was that they weren't always lecturing him or telling him that he was no good. As the waitress hurriedly brought the food to the table, one of the women mentioned to Kenneth that he had better go wash his hands, since he had gotten them greasy when he placed the bike in the car. Kenneth excused himself to go to the restroom. As he got out of his chair, Helen was looking in her purse for the bottle containing the cocktail of drugs.

As soon as he was out of sight, Helen poured some of her concoction into Kenneth's drink. When he returned and sat down, the women raised their glasses in a toast. Quickly Kenneth grabbed his glass and lifted it high and Helen said, "May tomorrow be even a better day for Kenneth McDavid." Kenneth chugalugged the drink till the glass was empty. Helen's eyes were fixed on Kenneth's empty glass. She was no pharmacist, but she knew that Kenneth's legs would soon turn to rubber. They went through the motions of eating the dinner. Kenneth tried to express his appreciation to the women of what it meant to him to have his own apartment and all that Olga had done to make sure he had good food to eat. As his speech became more slurred, he had difficulty finding the right words to express what these two women meant to him.

Helen announced that it was time to go, and she told Olga to take care of the tab as Helen escorted Kenneth to the car. Helen was holding on to Kenneth's elbow and pointed him to the parking lot. She knew if they stayed any longer there was no way that she and Olga could carry Kenneth to the car. As she reached the Sable, she opened the back door and told Kenneth to take a seat. By this time Kenneth's head was spinning around without knowing what was up and what was down. As Kenneth settled in the back seat, he leaned over and seemed to collapse onto his bicycle that had been placed next to him.

Olga came out and looked at Kenneth, who seemed to have passed out in the back seat. Helen told Olga to get in and they had to leave since it was past 9:00 p.m. Helen said that she didn't want to use the La Brea alley again since the police might be able to connect the two hit-and-runs. Helen explained that she had found a place in the Westwood area, an alley behind a Ross Clothing store where it was dark and isolated. Olga said she had no preference as long as they didn't get caught.

CHAPTER 4 CRUISING THE SUNSET STRIP

Helen made a few turns and was headed westbound on Sunset Boulevard. She had to stop at Laurel Canyon, which gave her an opportunity to test Olga's reminiscence skills by asking Olga which building was the Schwab's Drug Store. Olga pointed across the street and said that it had been torn down. She further stated that it wasn't really where Lana Turner was discovered. Helen indicated that she thought it was at Schwab's. Although they were not exactly arguing with each other, Helen tried to remember what was so legendary about Schwab's Drug Store.

As she drove across Laurel Canyon Boulevard, she could see directly in front of her the Chateau Marmont, which was all lit up. She told Olga that it always made her sad when she went by the Chateau, where John Belushi overdosed on speedballs (combination of heroin and cocaine) in bungalow #3, which is attached to the Chateau. Olga reminded her that the woman who gave him the speedball only got three years in prison for killing the comic. What an injustice! (On March 5, 1982, Kathy Smith, a backup singer from Canada, pleaded No Contest to supplying drugs to Belushi and received a sentence of three years in State prison)

Helen had started to drive down the Sunset Strip, which certainly looked more appealing at night when the bright lights covered up the aging facades of buildings that had so many tales to tell if they could talk. Sunset Boulevard weaves along the foothills of the Hollywood Hills, and there is an endless supply of young people standing outside various night clubs. Within a short distance Helen could see the outline of the House of Blues. Helen tried to show that she knew more show business trivia than Olga. She told Olga that she had heard that Phil Spector had picked up an actress at that House of Blues. Olga mused that she would never have fallen for the line 'Come over to my place for a drink.' Olga questioned what was the victim thinking and added that Spector even looked guilty based on his mug shot that had been published in the newspaper. (This author's book *Killing in the Castle* about the Spector case began here at the House of Blues).

Helen realized that she shouldn't have taken Sunset Boulevard, since traffic was beginning to become congested, although it was fun traveling down memory lane where all the nightclubs were located on both sides of the street during the 1950s and 60s. When Helen saw the Comedy Store come into view on the right-hand side, she had to remind Olga that it was originally Ciro's nightclub. She claimed she remembered when Frank Sinatra performed there.

Olga quipped back by saying that was where the stripper, Lil St. Cyr, was arrested in 1951, for showing too much of herself in the translucent bathtub and bubble bath. (Olga was correct in that two burly deputy Sheriffs testified they were **horrified** that Lil St. Cyr appeared to be nude, so after her performance they arrested her. At trial the stripper testified she had undergarments on which were nude in color. The jury deliberated for an hour and acquitted her. Thus began the rumor that the LA County DA's Office couldn't win the big cases.)

These two septuagenarians seemed to enjoy trying to outsmart the other as to what they remembered of the good old days on the Sunset Strip. Helen seemed to relive her younger years when she occasionally cruised down Sunset Boulevard. As she approached the 9000 block, she slowed down and looked up and down. She was parallel to the modern building of the Key Club, and she pointed her hand to the right. She said to Olga, "That's it." She explained that was where Mickey Cohen had his night club, Sherry's. That was before Olga had arrived in America from Hungary, so Helen had one up on Olga. Olga asked, "Who was Mickey Cohen?" This pleased Helen to no end since it proved she knew more about Hollywood than Olga, who had lived there for 30 years.

She exclaimed, "You don't remember when back in the late 1940s he was a mob boss who ran Hollywood and the Westside of LA?" She pointed to the curb and said that was where Mickey was standing when another mob boss tried to assassinate him in front of his night club. Olga showed disinterest since she didn't consider mobsters as being the real celebrities of Hollywood.

The heavy traffic was frustrating Helen, so she kept looking for a street that would take her down to Santa Monica Boulevard. Helen could make out the street sign that said "Doheny Drive." Helen pulled over into the left-hand lane and waited for her chance to turn and started down the hill. Olga wanted to top Helen, so she pointed to the left and couldn't help blurting out, "Marilyn Monroe lived there and Joe DiMaggio visited her there before they were married." Helen didn't miss a beat by firing back that wasn't important since the house Marilyn died in was way over in Brentwood.

As soon as Helen reached Santa Monica Boulevard, she had to halt for the red signal. Her head turned to the left and she could barely make out the sign for the

Troubadour night club at 9081 Santa Monica Boulevard, West Hollywood. She said to Olga, "Look, that's the Troubadour, where Lenny Bruce was arrested for using the word 'Schmuck.'" That event occurred in October 1962 when Deputy Sheriffs arrested Bruce for using obscene language in his comedy routine. The DA's Office tried him and all 12 jurors couldn't agree on a verdict, so it resulted in a hung jury and the case was never retried. Later, Bruce was convicted of using obscenities in New York and he was sentenced to four months in jail. Helen was elated that Olga didn't remember any of that.

When the signal turned green, Helen made a right and headed back through Beverly Hills. Helen asked Olga to look at Kenneth to see if he was completely knocked out. Olga checked him and replied, "He's Three Sheets to the Wind." (This was a rating system of inebriation among sailors. One Sheet meant Tipsy; two Sheets meant Intoxicated; three Sheets meant completely Unconscious.) Helen thought that was a strange response but kept on driving. Within five minutes she saw again the angel Moroni on top of the Mormon Temple. That reminded her that she needed to turn right on Westwood Boulevard. It was approaching 11:00 p.m. when Helen arrived at the Bristol Market where she made a left and almost immediately made another hard left to go down the alley.

CHAPTER 5 LOOKING FOR A DARK ALLEY

Helen firmly grabbed the Mercury Sable's steering wheel and turned down a lonely dark alley. She unhurriedly drove past the Bristol Market parking area. Only a few local residents were finishing up their grocery shopping. The alley was seldom used since its main purpose was for delivery trucks during the day to drop off merchandise. The headlights of the Mercury Sable were the only form of illumination of the alley. None of the businesses that backed up to the alley had any form of security lighting. Helen slowed the car to a crawl and inched her way further down the alley. She was nearly mid-block and through the rear view mirror she couldn't see the market parking lot any longer. She gently pulled to the left and drove a few feet, then stopped the car as far to the left as she could.

Fumbling for the light switch, she found the right one and the headlights went off while leaving on the interior lights. Helen told Olga to get out and she exited the driver's side. These two elderly ladies walked to the rear of the car. Helen had some difficulty in finding the button to open the rear door. Finally, it rose up and the two ladies pulled out the bicycle, which hit the pavement with a clunk. With both of them pulling on the bike, they were able to drag it over to the west side of the alley. Olga went back to the car and removed the helmet, and Helen pulled out the front tire. They neatly placed them in a pile close to the fences on the west side of the alley.

Then Helen opened the back door and the two women together reached in and grabbed some part of Kenneth's clothing and they yanked and pulled. He was heavier than they thought. Since he had passed out on the mixture of drugs, his body resembled Jell-O and it was like pulling dead weight. Unceremoniously, they pulled his body until it plopped onto the alley floor. They tried to drag him so his body would be placed in the center of the alley. It wasn't perfect, but it was close enough. Helen then asked Olga if she was certain that he had remembered to bring along his identification. Olga replied she had told him to bring along his wallet with his identification.

Helen wasn't buying Olga's explanation. She told her to check his pockets to be certain that he had something on him that had his address with his name. Olga disliked being dictated to by Helen, but she begrudgingly complied and reached into his pants back pocket and pulled out an old wallet. She could see it had several dollars in it. She flipped through, looking for some form of identification and came to a Visa card with his name and a California Identification card with his photo, name, and address on it.

Olga held it up in the air so Helen could see it. Olga said, "See, I told you so." Helen thought, why does Olga have to be this way? Didn't Olga remember in the Paul Vados situation that they had to file a Missing Persons report because the police didn't know who the victim was since he had no identification? The coroner had listed Paul as a 'John Doe,' and it took longer for the insurance companies to make the payouts since they required a death certificate in the victim's name. They also had to have a police report with Paul's name on it showing he was accidentally killed.

Helen was satisfied but she wished she didn't have to put up with Olga's stubborn attitude of being less than agreeable. Didn't Olga understand that this was merely a business deal in which everything had to be done right in order for their investment to pay off? Since it was so dark, Helen wanted to make sure that Kenneth McDavid was properly laid out in the alley. After checking to be sure everything was in place, Helen walked over to the driver's door and got in. Olga, not wanting to be left behind, jumped into the passenger side. Helen started the engine and turned the headlights back on, put the car in reverse, and backed up about 50 feet. She knew that the car had to have enough momentum to go over the body and not merely have a tire push it out of the way. Helen had lined up the Mercury Sable so she would strike the victim and the tires would run over him and thereby crush him to death.

Helen had the headlights facing down the alley. She could see that Kenneth was lying perpendicular to the alley and that everything looked right. Helen personally had made so many insurance premium payments on Kenneth's life that she didn't think of him as a human being but an investment about to pay off. Helen now could only see a homeless man lying in the alley. In her mind, a homeless person wasn't classified as a human being since he had no family. When Helen and Olga first met him at the Presbyterian homeless shelter, he was miserable. He was sleeping out of cardboard boxes and climbing in trash dumpsters behind restaurants looking for food. These homeless men would be better off dead because they would no longer have to endure such a miserable way of life.

Helen rationalized that she and Olga had given Kenneth a comfortable existence for many months. In other words, they had given him a good and happy send-off. As

Helen gunned the engine, the Sable lurched forward and she gripped the steering wheel with both hands. She didn't want the car to just push his body down the alleyway. As the car raced forward, she made sure that she squarely hit Kenneth dead center, thereby crushing him to death. She could feel his body become twisted and mangled beneath the undercarriage of the car. Helen and Olga heard and felt a thud under the floorboard as the car drove over Kenneth, seemingly to drag his body beneath the undercarriage of the car for a short distance. At some point the body seemed to become dislodged from under the car and the car jolted forward.

Helen moved her foot over to the brake pedal to get better control of the car. She wanted to slow down as she approached one of the cross streets that the alley passed over. Helen drove the car slowly and cautiously, crossing over the street to the other side of the alley. As she entered the alley on the other side, she pressed down on the accelerator and there was no response. Again she pushed her entire foot on the accelerator and nothing happened. The two women glanced at each other. Olga said, "Hurry up, let's get out of here."

Helen didn't know what to say as the car was merely coasting down the decline of the alley. Olga insisted that they needed to get out of there right NOW. The engine had completely stopped and Helen was fighting to control the steering wheel as they approached the end of the alley. Headlights remained on; however, they seemed to be moving in slow motion. She frantically grabbed the steering wheel with all her strength and turned the Sable to the left as they coasted into a Chevron Service Station parking area.

The following graphic page shows the alley where the victim McDavid was run over.

Graphic 2

GOLAY & RUTTERSCHMIDT CASE

June 21, 2005
Accident Scene

Alley showing where victim McDavid was run over.

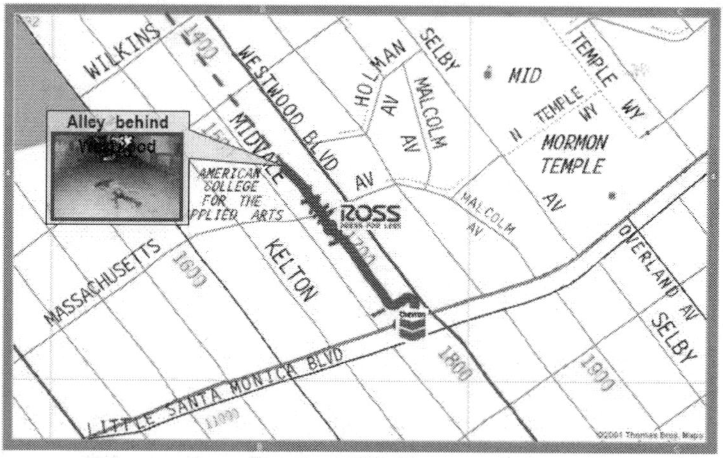

This map shows the alley which the suspects drove down.

CHAPTER 6 ACCIDENTS DO HAPPEN

The Sable vehicle seemed to gently glide into the service station, where it came to a stop. No noise was coming from the engine as Helen pressed firmly on the brakes. Helen was in a state of shock and needed some breathing room. Unfortunately, she was harassed by Olga yelling at her telling her she needed to learn how to drive a car. Helen's ashen face appeared that she was having a heart attack. Olga was berating her for being so cheap to pay only $6,000 for this used Sable. Olga went on saying that she knew there was something wrong with the car when they were buying it. By this time, Olga had become so agitated that she wasn't making any sense in her vile comments. Helen didn't respond to Olga's diatribe but looked around to see if she was clear of the alley. The idea was to get the car as far away as they could from the crime scene.

Many thoughts went through Helen's and Olga's minds. Olga had reverted to her typical self of blaming others. All she could think about was how to get away from the area without anyone connecting her to the accident. Yet Helen's mind was focused on assessing the situation and figuring out how to repair the car. Helen had

had few problems with her Mercedes SUV; however, with her other cars she had called the Auto Club for their roadside assistance services.

Helen started fumbling through her purse, but since it was dark in the car she stepped outside. She plunked her purse on top of the hood and started rummaging through it. She stuck her hand in and pulled out her wallet. She flipped it open and thumbed through her plastic cards. She passed over a number of credit cards. Eventually, she located her gray and blue Southern California Auto Club card. In the upper right-hand corner was the Roadside and Battery Service number listing an 800 phone number. She immediately punched that number into her cell phone and within a minute she had an operator who was asking questions such as what was the problem with the car and where was the car located. Helen had no difficulty with that question as to the location since she knew she was on the northwest corner of Westwood Boulevard and Santa Monica Boulevard.

This was a well-known intersection for people who had lived in the area a long time. This was the location for the Keg Liquor store that every old-time UCLA student was familiar with. The reason was this was the nearest place that alcohol could be purchased. When UCLA was founded, there was an agreement that no liquor store could be within so many miles of the campus. The Keg Liquor store was exactly the appropriate distance away from campus. No Greek party occurred on fraternity row without some member driving to the Keg to pick up several kegs for the parties. Helen remembered how important the Keg Liquor store was but that when the University requirements were relaxed, the store went out of business and a Chevron service station replaced it.

Finally, the auto club operator continued to ask what was wrong with the car. Helen knew that she couldn't explain to the operator that she was in the process of running over someone when the engine died. Helen was smart enough not to tell the truth but merely generalize that the car suddenly stopped running and that she had no idea what caused it. She indicated that the car may need to be towed to Santa Monica.

The operator said they would have a tow truck there in 20 minutes. Helen turned to Olga and said, "OK, we will get a tow in 20 minutes." Olga started complaining that the tow trucks were never on time and that it would be an hour before it got there. Olga wanted to get out of the area and told Helen she would call a friend to pick her up or call for a taxi. Olga continued to complain as she walked over to the service station office and disappeared from view.

Helen knew the tow truck operator would need to see her Auto Club card, so she didn't put it away in her wallet. Helen was curious if there was any damage to the Sable, so she walked around to survey any auto body dents connected to the accident. She stooped down as low as she could to look at the undercarriage of the car. She was pleased there was no apparent damage she could see.

At her age she didn't like to have too much excitement that could affect her heart. As she stood by the side of the car, she could feel her heart pounding. She didn't want to pass out and wished she had brought some Xanax along to calm herself down. Here she was, standing next to the 'Killer Car' just two blocks from the alley where a dead body was lying. As of yet she hadn't seen any police cars or ambulances responding to the area of the alley. So far, there was no sound of sirens that might indicate the body had been discovered. Throughout her life she had been in difficult situations and she had always had the smarts to slither out of whatever difficulty she had found herself in.

Her mind was twirling in circles and she tried to concentrate on one thing at a time. She knew for survival's sake she needed to get this car as far away from the crime scene as possible. What should she tell the tow truck operator? Should she admit that this was her car, or should she use the name of the woman they had used to purchase the car? Helen couldn't remember what the lady's name was. She remembered that Olga had the lady's driver's license, which they had stolen from a gym where the woman was working out. The woman lived somewhere in Encino in the San Fernando Valley. Maybe it would be better if Helen claimed that she was merely borrowing the car and leave it at that.

As she stood by the Sable waiting for the tow truck, she could see dozens of drivers pull into the service station and stop at the gas pumps. It was an enormous service station with multi-pumps. She noticed a well-dressed woman in a Mercedes exit her car and walk over to the pumps and put her credit card in and then remove the nozzle. She lifted it with effort and seemed to wrestle with the nozzle to place it in the fuel spout. That lady stepped slightly to the side so she wouldn't spill any gasoline on her outfit. From this lady's stiletto heels all the way to fashionable hairdo, she was dressed to kill. As she waited for the tank to fill, she was on her cell phone chatting about whatever was important at that very moment in her life.

Helen smiled to herself and thought that could have been her when she was younger and on the prowl. Then she slowly shook her head and thought that would never have been her. When Helen was that gal's age in the 1950s she would pull into a service station and an attendant would come out in a spotless uniform and ask her, "Ma'am, Standard or Ethyl?" To impress the attendant she would say, "Of course, Ethyl." Then he would start the pump going as he danced around the car, opening up the hood to check the oil and water. Then he would waltz over to the driver's window holding the oil lipstick to show the level of the oil. He would ask, "28 or 32?" Since Helen liked a softer ride, she would reply, "28 please." After he closed the hood he automatically took his air gauge out to check every tire to make sure it had exactly 28 pounds of pressure. The final encore of the attendant's performance was when he grabbed a wet sponge and started cleaning the windshield as well as the rear window. After the gas tank was full he came by and said, "That will be $2.50."

Helen longed for those good old days when there was **real service** in service stations. But what she liked most was those gas prices such as .23 cents per gallon. Helen saw the young lady return the nozzle in the pump, but she could barely make out the total gas charge of $68.00. The lady reentered her little Mercedes coupe and sped off.

Helen, having relived all the nostalgia, didn't notice the tow truck pull into the service station from the Westwood Boulevard side. As soon as she saw the tow truck she snapped back into reality and she stood on her tippy toes and waved her hands to get the tow truck driver's attention. Helen, being short in stature, didn't stand out. She stepped to the side of the car and waved her purse in the air, which attracted the tow truck operator's attention.

CHAPTER 7 NEED A TOW

The tow truck operator pulled up and seemed to recognize that Helen was like a 'damsel in distress.' He parked adjacent to the Sable and jumped out with his clipboard in his hand. Helen went up to the tow operator and in her most coy, helpless voice explained she didn't know what was wrong with the car. He asked if the car's battery worked and she indicated that it was running fine and all of a sudden the engine went dead. She didn't think it was necessary to tell him the details as to how and why the engine stopped. He asked for the keys and Helen handed them to him. He plunked himself down and tried to start the engine. The starter turned the engine over, but the engine wouldn't catch. By then the operator had eliminated the battery and starter as being the problem. He checked the gas gauge and saw it was half full, so it wasn't out of gas.

He looked at his watch and saw it was 1:00 a.m. and advised Helen that something was wrong with the engine. Helen knew that but she wanted it repaired. He said the Ford agencies were all closed but he could tow it to one of the agencies and leave it in their driveway. Helen could contact them in the morning. He said he could drop the car at any garage if she had one in mind. She said she wasn't familiar with any of the garages in the Westwood area. She suggested, "Why don't you tow the Sable to my place in Santa Monica and I will take care of the problem tomorrow?"

The tow driver said, "What's the address?" Helen explained it was Ocean Park, in Santa Monica. He took her Auto Club membership card and copied down the basic information and had her sign and gave her a copy. He pulled his tow truck around, backed up, and hooked up the car. Helen in her most charming way asked if he could permit her to ride in the tow truck with him to her house. He said, "OK, if you don't mind riding in a tow truck." Helen realized that her options were limited, so she enthusiastically agreed.

Within five minutes, Helen climbed into the tall tow truck and settled back for a jolting ride to her house. They pulled out onto Santa Monica Boulevard heading west. Helen wasn't used to riding so high in a truck. She had a different perspective as she gawked out the window at a city that looked better after dark, when all the bright lights cover up the urban blight.

As they approached Purdue Street, the signal turned red and she could feel the weight of the Sable pushing against the tow truck. She glanced to the left and could see the LAPD station, which looked peaceful with police cars parked in front. She thought to herself as to whether anyone had spotted McDavid's body and had called this station to report the incident. Next to the police station was the old West Los Angeles courthouse where Helen remembered standing in long lines just to shell out money for a parking ticket. Those weren't fond memories but recollections of other interesting times.

When the signal turned green she could feel the tow truck struggle forward. All she could see were fast food restaurants that seemed to be a bustling with business after midnight. Cars packed the drive-through lanes with drivers impatient to get their burgers and fries. She pondered how much things had changed from her high school days in Washington State where she was introduced to the Dairy Queen. The food was wholesome and cooked to order and not kept warm for hours under heat lamps. She thought how nice cherry malt would taste right now.

The tow truck operator certainly hadn't won any awards for Mr. Personality or Most Congenial, so Helen decided not to make any 'small talk.' His main concern was how fast he could take off from one signal to get to the next signal. He seemed to be involved in his own race to get to Helen's place as fast as humanly possible. He had his radio blaring out additional calls for tow services. In the background he had the police scanner on. So far, there was no mention of a hit-and-run in the Westwood alley.

Since Helen had asked a favor to ride with the tow operator, she didn't feel comfortable telling the driver how to get to her house. He turned left off of Santa Monica Boulevard onto Fourth Street; that wouldn't be the route Helen would have used. She hated going down Fourth Street since it reminded her of the Farmers Market Massacre that occurred on July 16, 2003. She felt lucky that she hadn't been at the outdoor market on that fateful day. An elderly man, George Weller, who was 86 years old, was leaving the post office when he drove by the entrance to the Farmers Market. For whatever reason, he accidentally stepped on the accelerator and plowed into dozens of shoppers. His Buick vehicle barreled through vegetable stands, throwing bodies in the air and driving over others. By the time the dust settled 10 individuals were dead and 63 were seriously injured.

This tragedy left this liberal city of Santa Monica demanding justice. The DA's Office prosecuted the elderly driver and ultimately convicted him of 10 counts of Vehicular Manslaughter. Then the community was torn apart. Some wanted the elderly man to spend the rest of his life in prison and others wanted him to lose his license and remain under house arrest. Finally, it was worked out that his sentence was probation. However, because of the seriousness of the injuries and the deaths, it was decided that it was the fault of the city of Santa Monica in that they hadn't put in enough permanent barriers to prevent a car from crashing inside the makeshift farmers market. It cost the city over 21 million dollars and now there are concrete barriers all around the streets where the Farmers Market is held.

Helen didn't like to drive by the area since it reminded her of how dangerous it was when a car drives over bodies. Within minutes the tow truck was in front of her house. There were no parking places near Helen's house. But one block over there was a vacant space and the tow truck operator was able to position and drop the Sable into the parking space. After he unhitched everything the tow truck driver was off on another call. It was almost 2:00 a.m. as Helen climbed the stairs to her house. As she entered her house, she shook her head as to what a rough day it had been merely killing someone to collect on the life insurance. All the unexpected mechanical problems with the 'Killer Car' made for a full day.

The next day was busy in that she had to call someone to come out and fix the car. She didn't want to know what had to be done. All Helen wanted was to have the Sable running again. It took her mechanic friend a few days to figure out what was wrong and then using an alligator clamp he reattached the fuel line, which had become detached. Helen was pleased she could drive the car over to the alley behind her house. She parked it alongside the apartment building directly behind her house. This had been a regular parking space for one of the apartment residents. Notes were placed on the windshield of the Sable by the resident asking the owner to move the car away. Helen could be stubborn at times and felt that she was a taxpayer and she had just as much right to park in the public alley as the apartment dwellers.

Now to return to the crime scene the night of the incident around 1:00 a.m., Yoram Hassid was playing backgammon with his friends Masoud Kaufman (pseudonym) and Behrooz Haven (pseudonym) at a local furniture store on Westwood Boulevard. When the game was over he said good-bye to his friends and left. Since he had parked to the rear of the store in the alley, he went to his car and proceeded southbound down the alley. His headlights came upon what appeared to be something suspicious in the alley. He immediately put the car in reverse and backed up all the way to the rear of the store. He ran into the store and told his friends what he had seen.

He exclaimed, "Close the door, there's a body lying in the alley." The men didn't know what to think or what they should do. Finally, the store owner, Kaufman, decided he would leave with his other friend Haven to slowly drive his car down the alley. There were no lights that shined down on the alley, and all they had for illumination was the headlights of his car. As the car moved closer, they were seated in the front and were leaning forward with their foreheads almost touching the windshield to see what their friend had told them. The best they could determine was that it looked like a body lying in the alley with some type of bicycle lying next to it.

Mr. Kaufman, the owner of the store, felt obligated to contact someone about this situation. He dialed 9-1-1 and a police dispatcher came on the phone. He described seeing a body lying in the alley not moving. The response from the 9-1-1 operator was to tell him to honk the horn to see if the person responded. Every night the dispatcher receives numerous calls of people lying drunk and passed out on the ground. The men honked their horn continuously and watched to see if the body moved.

The figure looked like a man with greasy clothes on that didn't seem to wake up or move. The two men looked at each other, and without saying a word both wondered, what did we get ourselves into? The operator didn't want to send a police unit out at that hour just because some drunk had passed out in an alley. The person in the alley wasn't causing a disturbance. The dispatcher remained calm and wondered how she could elicit some civic assistance from the caller. She wanted these men to save some time for the police by merely pulling the drunk to a safe place and letting him sleep it off.

The driver got the hint and finally mustered up enough nerve to get out of the car and see if he could wake up the drunk. As he proceeded a little closer he could see that the man had on a pair of glasses. It was hard to obtain a clear view, since the headlights seemed to create more shadows than illumination. As he approached closer, he noticed the color red near the man's head. Could that be blood? He leaned down to touch the dirty face and there was no feeling of life. He returned to the car and reported his finds to the dispatcher, who sent out a police unit that arrived within minutes.

As the days passed, Helen continued to be unpopular with her neighbors. The Santa Monica apartment residents who lived behind her took their parking spaces seriously. The warning notices were more compelling to move this damn Sable out of the alley. Someone took red paint and threw it against the tires. There are people who might consider this vandalism, but Helen recognized what she was up against, so one evening she moved the Sable. It ended up being parked on the street two blocks from Olga's apartment in Hollywood. Helen left it abandoned there.

The parking enforcement wrote three parking citations. The Sable sat for weeks until the police tow truck picked it up and parked it in the police impound lot. Since no one claimed the Sable, it was sold at a police auction, where a young couple purchased it for their main means of transportation. They were unaware this was a 'Killer Car' and they thought they had made a financial killing in purchasing the Sable at the police auction.

On the following graphic page is the map showing where the Mercury Sable was towed to Helen Golay's place in Santa Monica. Included is the check Golay paid for her Auto Club fee, listing the membership number which matches the dispatcher's log regarding the tow.

Graphic 3

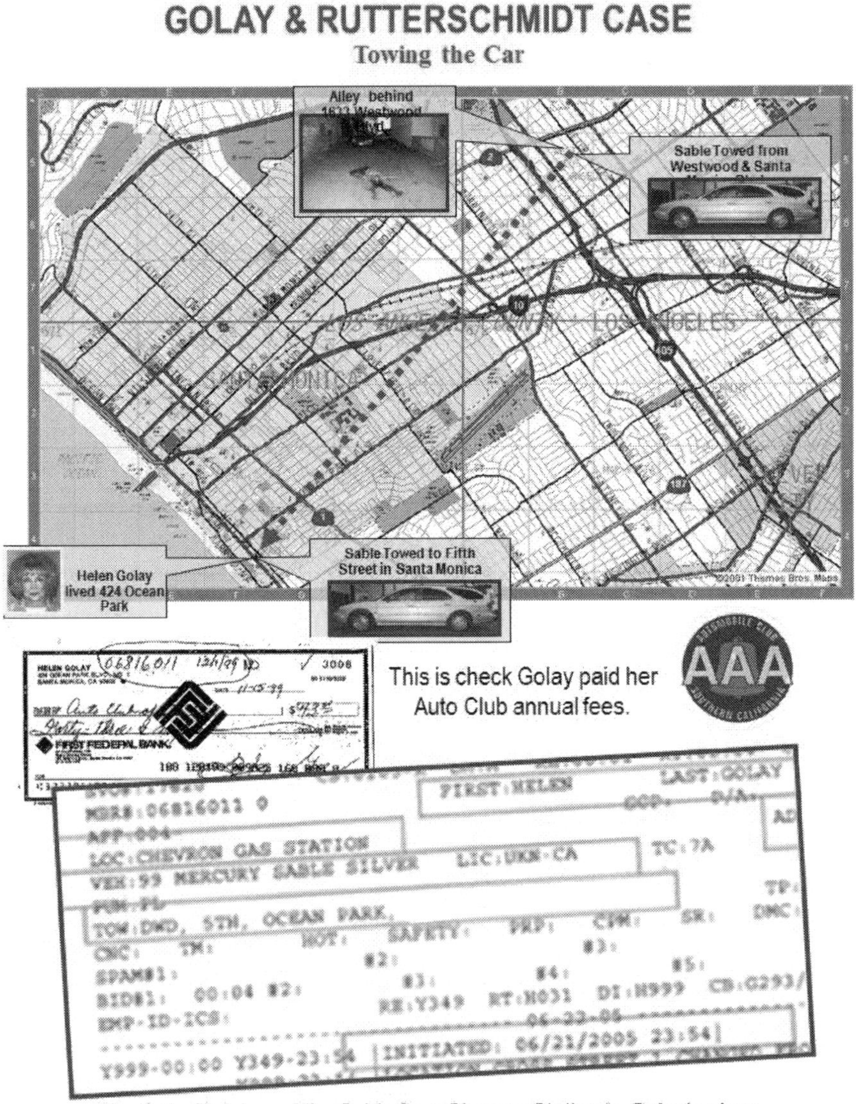

The Auto Club towed the Sable from Chevron Station to Golay's place.

CHAPTER 8 WHO IS HELEN GOLAY?

Helen Louise Salisbury was born on February 3, 1931, in Eastland, Texas. Her father died in a traffic accident when she was very young. As a result, she grew up with various family members and eventually lived with a foster care family. She moved to Hoquiam, Washington, where she lived with a foster family. She excelled at Hoquiam High School and was on the honor roll and a member of the Spanish Club. After high school she moved to California.

She met and married Vernon Golay and had two daughters. After eight years the union terminated in a divorce. Years later he retired as a dentist living in Oregon and never had any contact with Helen. Helen met and married a David Wells and they had one daughter. But for various reasons the marriage lasted merely a year. He was an engineer in Orange County.

It wasn't clear as to when Helen started working for Douglas Aircraft at Clover Field in Santa Monica. This company was founded by Donald Douglas Sr. in 1921. He had been the first person to circumnavigate the world by air in 1924. Douglas Aircraft was well known for building sturdy commercial aircraft like the DC-2 followed by the DC-3 in 1936, which was the plane that truly started air travel for the masses. There are DC-3 planes that are still flying today in remote areas of the world.

During WWII, Douglas Aircraft joined with other aircraft manufacturers and formed the Boeing-Vega-Douglas consortium to produce the B-17 Flying Fortress. This group of companies ended up producing some 30,000 aircraft from 1942 to 1945. After the war, the workforce of 160,000 was sharply reduced, but many of the employees continued working on the commercial Douglas DC-8. Helen was there during that phase as well as when the company expanded to develop the NASA projects involving the Saturn rockets. Her co-workers remember Helen as the type who wanted to be noticed either by how she dressed or flirting with her bosses.

As Douglas experienced layoffs and cutbacks in the late 1980s, Helen decided to spread her wings and go out on her own as a real estate agent in Santa Monica. Since she had lived in Santa Monica for so long, she was familiar with every part of this beach community. Besides earning large commissions, she also learned about probate sales. As a result, in time she bought probate property and held it as an investment. This allowed her to grow a nest egg for her later years.

Helen became a schemer in business dealings and she learned some questionable ways to make money. Through her dealings she came in contact with an older gentleman, Fred Downie, who was injured in an auto accident. Helen tried to help him and somehow talked him into giving her Power of Attorney. Magically, she obtained title to his house. She sold his house, making $200,000. Apparently, she learned early on how to deal with old men and manipulate them to sign documents for her benefit.

Along those lines, Helen told her hairdresser that she was thinking of marrying an elderly man, and that after the wedding she would give him all the Viagra he wanted and eventually he would have a heart attack and die. As a result, she would end up with all his money. How serious Helen was is not known. She relished making money in an unorthodox way. One of her scams was to create a pyramid of credit cards in which one credit card company would take the big loss.

Possibly from her real estate experience she learned the mastery of suing people and companies. In one incident, she sued a woman claiming that the woman hadn't returned a leather skirt she owned. In another civil lawsuit Helen sued a gym, claiming that she was injured on the gym exercise equipment. On several occasions, she and her investment partner, Olga Rutterschmidt, joined in lawsuits against markets and stores claiming that boxes had fallen on either of them and forcing the companies to settle the cases.

As a matter of fact, Helen even sued her daughter, Karen (pseudonym) and her boyfriend. Most of the time Helen and her daughter had a good relationship, but she wanted her to marry a wealthy man who would be able to support his new mother-in-law, Helen, in a manner she would like. In the end, her daughter and boyfriend countersued her for being deceitful. This lawsuit created bad blood in the Golay family.

It wasn't that Helen was a pauper. She had a house near the beach that was worth more than $1.5 million. As a matter of fact, at the time of her arrest in this case, the feds were able to seize $1.2 million in cash from her bank accounts. She always enjoyed driving around town in her expensive Mercedes SUV.

Over the years, Helen gained wisdom and she explained, "I have learned that men are STUPID and renters are PIGS." But what was most important to Helen was her appearance. When she was younger, she could turn heads, but as the years accumulated she required some plastic surgery to maintain her looks. By the time of her arrest, a journalist described Helen as "A lady with a reddish bouffant and dyed blond locks, liberally applied make-up, loads of eyeliner, bright lipstick, and tight-fitting flashy clothes." She was proud of her plastic surgery and her expression was, "Every mature woman needs a little help fighting the gravity resettling process."

During Helen's original appearances in court, she demanded that her attorney ask the judge for permission for her to possess in jail tweezers so she could pluck her eyebrows. Also, she requested that she have her own makeup to be used before each of her court appearances. However, by the end of the trial Helen requested the judge to permit her to wear thermal underwear and a special diet for her high blood pressure. Her attorney begged the judge to treat her like a human being. In fairness to her attorney, he never asked the judge to treat her like a **DECENT** human being.

CHAPTER 9 WHO IS OLGA RUTTERSCHMIDT?

Olga was born in Hungary on March 5, 1933, and grew up and attended high school there. Olga was seven years old at the beginning of WWII, and Hungary was under German control. After the war, the Russians maintained control of Hungary, installing their own Communist government. However, on October 23, 1956, a student demonstration escalated as it marched to the Parliament building. The security forces fired on the students, which became one of the shortest and fiercest revolutions in European history. It lasted a mere 17 days until the Soviet Union realized that it couldn't afford to let the Eastern European countries withdraw from the Warsaw Pact. Consequently, the Soviet troops marched into Hungary with their tanks and brutally crushed the revolt.

The result was that thousands of Hungarians fled their country. The USA took in many of the immigrants. Olga was one of those immigrants who came to America in 1957. Olga ended up in the Los Angeles area and married another Hungarian, Endre Rutterschmidt. In order to survive, they bought a coffee shop in downtown LA, which they operated for years. As a couple, they had no children. Later they divorced and her husband returned to live in Hungary.

Olga continued to operate the coffee shop on her own but recognized it wasn't worth the hard work and long hours. She lived in an apartment on Sycamore Avenue for more than 30 years. She didn't have many friends and enjoyed playing her jazz and classical music loud. However, she was the first to complain if her neighbors tried to play their music louder than she liked. She was somewhat the 'hall monitor' for the apartment complex and she had no difficulty telling anyone off if they caused any problems around the complex.

For recreation Olga enjoyed hiking up Runyon Canyon, which was nearby. She would also take short road trips in her Honda Civic. She didn't seem to have any steady income. She liked to tell neighbors or friends that she could show them how to make easy money. Olga liked to discuss her pyramid of credit cards scheme. At any one time she would have 30 to 40 credit cards and end up defrauding all those credit card companies. She seemed to take delight in ripping off credit card companies. She would further explain that the money one made fleecing credit card companies was all tax-free.

She loved to sue businesses and would conjure up a fictitious scheme to sue them. In the early 1990s, she got into an argument at a coffee shop over a muffin she claimed was inedible. As a result, she sued the restaurant and one of the customers over the incident. Later, in 1997, she had refined her suing technique in that she claimed she was injured by falling light fixtures. Then she moved on to 'deeper pocket' companies and brought a suit against Ralph's Market for a stack of boxes falling on her.

Olga and Helen had a lot in common when they met at a Westside gym. They were both frequent visitors to the Beverly Hills Hotel and the Roosevelt Hotel in Hollywood. They worked as a pair. They would go into the restrooms of the hotels and change into a swimsuit and make complete use of the hotel's pool facilities. As they enjoyed the hotel's upscale ambience, they would have an eye out for purses or wallets left out at the pool area. This was small-time thievery which they were proud to get away with.

As a team they brought over 40 lawsuits against various businesses just to see how much they could make out of settlements. They truly could be called the most 'Litigious Septuagenarians' ever. Olga looked up to Helen since she had made the most from her property investments. Helen relied on Olga to scout out various business deals, and she would give Olga a commission if the deal worked out.

Helen and Olga had a strange relationship in that they didn't socialize together but were engaged in various business deals. Helen liked to dress in flashy clothes with a short skirt and plenty of make-up, while Olga dressed dowdy and spoke with a thick Hungarian accent. It was understandable as to how the two of them got the label as **'a poor man's version of the Gabor sisters.'**

CHAPTER10 HIT-AND-RUN INVESTIGATION

Such had to be done before Helen and Olga could collect on the life insurance policies. They made contact with each other and it was agreed that Helen would go to the Coroner's Office on Mission Road to obtain a death certificate and make arrangements for the cremation of Kenneth McDavid. On the other hand, Olga was assigned to go to LAPD, Wilshire Traffic Division, and asked for an accident report involving the death of Kenneth McDavid. Olga was referred to Detective Nelson Hernandez. Olga asked for an accident report, indicating that she was a relative of the victim.

Olga had never been interested in pursuing an acting career. That may have been a big mistake for both of them. Detective Hernandez handled dozens of Hit-and-Run cases, and the relatives who came in were always emotionally upset about the loss of their loved one. They had numerous questions they wanted to ask about the investigation and the likelihood of catching the hit-and-run drivers. Olga showed no emotion nor asked any questions about the investigation. All she wanted to know was how long it would take to get a copy of the police report. There was no feeling in her voice, just a matter-of-fact question indicating she would wait for the report.

Detective Hernandez couldn't get a handle on this McDavid case. He was bothered by the fact that the victim was found with a bike that hadn't been damaged. What appeared even stranger was that the front wheel was off the bike as though the victim was fixing a flat tire. Still, the problem was that the front tire wasn't flat. So why was the front tire off? The other question was, why didn't the victim walk down to the next street where there was plenty of light to work on the bike?

Also, Detective Hernandez received the Coroner's findings that the victim didn't have any broken legs. In the usual hit-and-run accident, the front of the car strikes the victim and knocks the victim to the side or flips him or her over the car. In both scenarios the victim almost always suffers broken bones. Here in McDavid's case, his entire rib cage was crushed and there was a tread mark on his jeans. The detective noticed so much grease on the victim's clothing which was more indicative of a car driving over the victim.

When the toxicology report came back from the Coroner, it seemed very abnormal that the report indicated that the victim had a substantial amount of Ambien in his system. This didn't make any sense. Why would a person take a sleep medication just before going on a bike ride? Detective Hernandez kept shaking his head since the facts didn't add up to the typical hit-and-run. He was perplexed as to what to do with the case.

The women were successful at their assigned task and had all the documents to send to the various insurance companies. Each company had a claim form that required certain information. Helen was good at filling out all these forms accompanied with the police report and death certificate. She mailed them off and waited for a check from each insurance company. Since all of the insurance policies were less than the requisite two years old, the companies could contest each of the policies. Since several of the policies were for large sums of money, several of the companies required additional information.

One insurance company was named MONY, and they employed investigator Ed Webster, who was assigned in New York. He wanted to check out the stories of the women since in one document the beneficiaries were listed as **business partners** and later they were **relatives**. The policy was for one million dollars, so the company thought it was worth looking into before paying out such a large amount. The NY investigator came to Los Angeles to meet with the women and to find out what was the reason for the different listing of the relationship of the parties. He went to their residences and they wouldn't talk to him. He left business cards explaining he needed to talk to them. They deliberately continued to avoid him. He couldn't understand why they didn't want to cooperate, since he wasn't going to pay without meeting with them.

This impasse went on for months. The investigator started contacting other insurance companies and learned that there were numerous life insurance policies under the name of Kenneth McDavid. In each of those policies the beneficiaries were either both of the women or one of them. Some of the policies were for the accidental death of McDavid and others were for term life insurance. By this time the private investigator, Ed Webster, decided to contact LAPD to see if there might be some type of fraud involving these two ladies.

It was in 2005, and one of the top TV shows that year was *Criminal Minds*. That series involved an elite group of profilers that analyze the dangerous criminal minds in an effort to anticipate their next moves before they would **strike again**. That TV program had similarities to the McDavid's case. Ed Webster met with Detective Hernandez and explained all the insurance policies the women had taken out on

Kenneth McDavid's life. All of a sudden the suspicion Detective Hernandez had about the McDavid case began to resurface. There was a fear that these women might **strike again**.

The other top TV program in 2005 was Numb3rs, which involved an FBI mathematician who uses equations to help solve various crimes. Maybe it was time to bring in the FBI. Detective Hernandez agreed that this was starting to look like a major fraud case. He decided to contact the FBI since this seemed to have the features of a Mail Fraud case, which is a federal crime since it crosses over state boundaries. It was uncanny how these TV series in 2005 were particularly relevant to the hit-and-run case of Kenneth McDavid.

CHAPTER 11 CONNECTING THE TWO CASES

Detective Hernandez was pleased that his suspicions weren't unfounded on his part. It was like big red flags were waving in the wind indicating that something was wrong about the so-called hit-and-run involving Kenneth McDavid. He was so amazed that these little old ladies might really be criminals and not 'do-gooders of the homeless.' Detective Hernandez was so flabbergasted and he wanted some of his fellow detectives to hear his story to validate his initial findings. Detective Lee Willmon worked in the cubical across from Hernandez in the same detective squad room. Detective Hernandez said, "Lee, you wouldn't believe the suspects in this hit-and-run I have been investigating." Lee replied, "What's the big deal?"

Then Det. Hernandez started explaining how this dude was supposedly the victim of a hit-and-run but nothing added up. These two old ladies apparently loaded up this homeless guy with life insurance policies, and after his death they tried to collect millions from the insurance companies. His desk mate said, "That sounds very familiar, I had a case like that almost five years ago involving a homeless guy and two old ladies who came by the station wanting a police report and claimed the body." Det. Hernandez said, "What did you do with the case?" Det. Willmon said he didn't know what to do with the case so he put it in the Cold Case files.

The phone rang, so the conversation between the two detectives terminated. Later in the day, Det. Willmon was walking by the cabinet containing Cold Case files. Out of curiosity, he opened it and thumbed through a number of old cases. He picked up the binder that had imprinted in bold numbers **1999.** He smiled to himself remembering how that was the year everyone was afraid of the 'Y2K Bug,' which was going to destroy all the computers that hadn't been programmed for another millennium. All that hype turned out to be much to do about nothing.

Then he thumbed through the reports until he came to the name of 'Paul Vados.' He remembered that was the old case he had worked on. He flipped it open to see who the old women were that asked for a copy of the police report. The victim, Paul Vados, had been run over on November 8, 1999, and it was a hit-and-run without any suspects. Then he leafed through the pages and saw the report with the names of the persons who had filed a missing person report; they were Helen Golay and Olga Rutterschmidt.

He returned to his desk with the old file in his hand. By this time his desk mate was off the phone and he asked, "What are the names of your old ladies?" As Det. Hernandez glanced for the names he said he remembered one was Helen and the other was a long German name. Det. Willmon said, "What about a Helen Golay and Olga Rutterschmidt?" Det. Hernandez shouted back in a loud excited voice, "That's them!"

The two detectives took both police reports and put them side by side to compare the facts. Everything was the same except for the date, the location, and victim's names. How fortuitous that the two detectives who sat across from each other had similar cases which occurred five years apart. For Det. Hernandez this confirmed that these two old ladies were involved in ripping off the insurance companies. Det. Willmon dusted off his old Cold Case and reopened it.

Based on the investigation, it appeared that these two old ladies had been scamming numerous insurance companies. Originally, the detectives had accepted the fact that these ladies were genuinely interested in helping the less fortunate homeless people in our society. These women were not as altruistic as people first thought. The detectives were astute enough to know they were on to something. Det. Hernandez looked at his watch to see what time it was in New York. He realized that he could still contact Ed Webster, the insurance investigator for the MONY insurance company, who was still in the office.

Det. Hernandez was able to reach Mr. Webster and asked if he was sitting down. Ed Webster jokingly said, "What have you come up with now?" Det. Hernandez said, "Ed you won't believe what I learned from my fellow detective whose desk is across from me." Webster was perplexed, not knowing where Det. Hernandez was going with this conversation. Det. Hernandez said, "Those two nice ladies did the same thing five years ago. The name of the victim was a Paul Vados and they claimed to be a cousin and a fiancé of him." Webster's reaction was, "You've got to be kidding me." Det. Hernandez asked Webster if he could check with the various insurance companies to see if there were numerous life insurance policies in the name of 'Paul Vados.' Webster agreed to check the name out and get back with them the next day as to what he found out.

The next day Det. Hernandez received a call back from Webster, who had found out there were over a dozen life insurance policies that Golay and Rutterschmidt had collected on for over $600,000. With this information it was clear that this was becoming a major fraud case.

The two detectives from the LAPD Westside **Traffic Division** recognized they didn't have the expertise to track down all the possible insurance policies with companies throughout the country. It was time to turn the matter over to the **FBI Insurance Fraud Division,** since they have the contacts and resources to obtain all the evidence to make a fraud case. What may have been the most interesting fact was that no one thought Helen and Olga were scam artists. These women took out numerous life insurance policies on homeless men who had health problems and knew they weren't likely to live for very long. The women knew the odds were in favor of these homeless men dying within a short time.

Some detectives with more suspicious minds wondered if these little old ladies could actually be involved in speeding up the deaths of the homeless men. Obviously, the police didn't really know what they had and how ruthless these little old ladies were! Could there be more similar cases? The investigation of a homeless man who was run over in a dark alley on June 21, 2005, was not the biggest news item at this time in the country. Shortly thereafter, on August 29, 2005, Hurricane Katrina slammed into New Orleans and other southern areas. The nation's attention was fixated on the Superdome and all the suffering that resulted from this tragedy. The investigation of the McDavid case slowed and the insurance companies were consumed by damage from the hurricane. This McDavid life insurance fraud case would just have to wait.

On the following graphic page is the information about the Paul Vados case which occurred five years earlier.

Graphic 4

KILLING OF PAUL VADOS
(November 8, 1999)

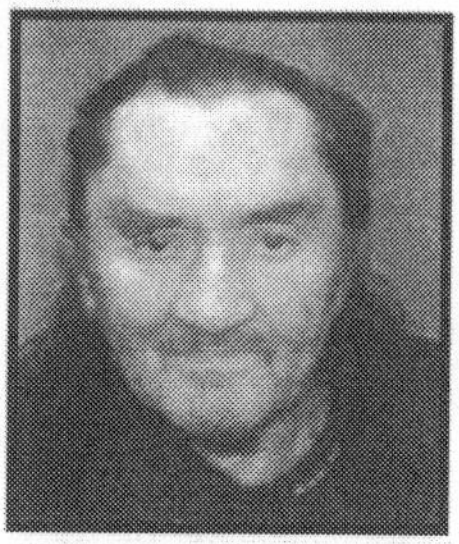

Paul Vados (73)

Location where Paul Vados was run over in alleyway

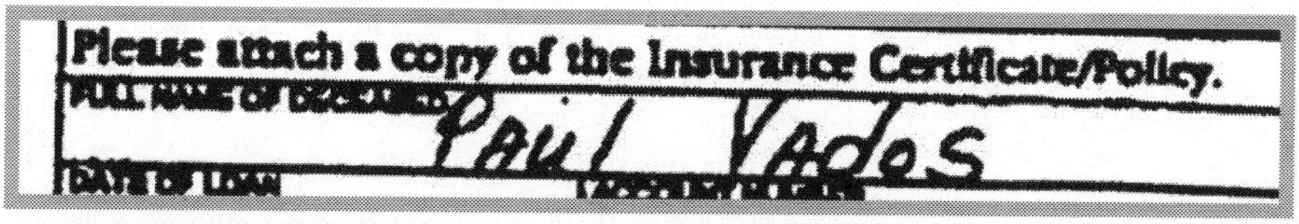

Please attach a copy of the Insurance Certificate/Policy.
FULL NAME OF DECEASED: Paul Vados
DATE OF LOAN

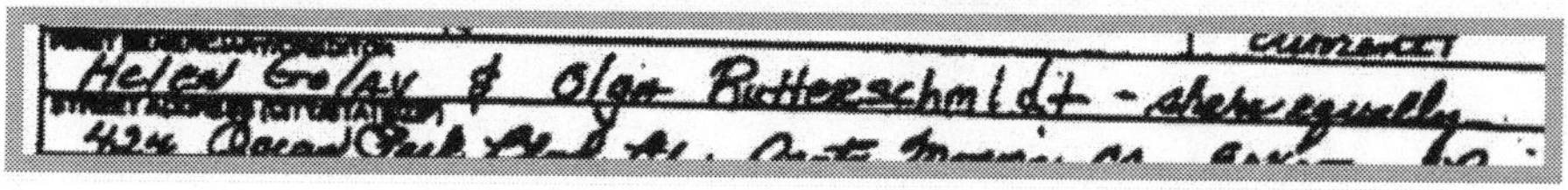

Helen Golay & Olga Rutterschmidt - share equally

Life Insurance policies taken out by suspects for victim Vados

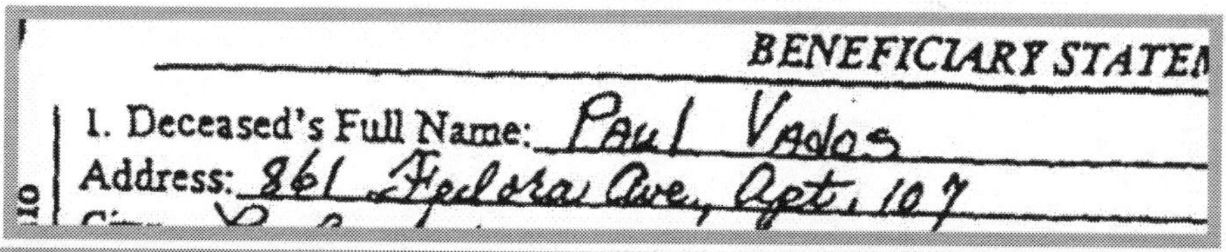

BENEFICIARY STATEM
1. Deceased's Full Name: Paul Vados
Address: 861 Fedora Ave, Apt. 107

fraudulent claim for the payment of a loss is guilty of a crime and may be subject to fines and confinement in state

Date: 1/4/2000 (60% of $30,000.–
Signature: Helen Golay as Beneficiary 60%
(Beneficiary, Executor, etc.)
SSN: 545-40-7950
Name: Helen Golay Address: 424 Ocean Pk
City: Santa Monica, CA. State: Santa Monica, CA Zip:

CHAPTER 12 SURVEILLANCE

What the investigators didn't know was how many other homeless men had the women taken out life insurance on? The other question was, what type of insurance policies were these? Were they accidental death policies or merely natural death policies? The insurance investigator was able to learn that some of them were accidental death type policies. This meant the victim would have to die from an accident and not from natural causes. In such situations, the victim would have to suffer an accidental death such as in a hit-and-run.

The police now knew that both victims in the two cases were killed in an accidental setting: to wit, run over by a vehicle in a dark alley. This would be a murder situation and not merely a mail fraud case. To be on the safe side, the LAPD administrators said that Robbery Homicide Division (RHD) should be contacted so they could participate in the investigation if the deaths were intentional. No one knew where this little fraud case might lead. Both LAPD and the FBI needed to learn the facts about the intentions of these women. All agreed that the two women should be placed under 24-hour surveillance to figure out what they were really up to.

Many people who watch TV programs depicting detectives think that this is an exciting job full of action. However, much of a detective's day is consumed by pursuing clues that lead to nothing more than a dead end. Especially, doing surveillance work requires the 'Patience of Job.' Many hours are spent sitting in a car watching for a suspect to make a move. Some suspects are next to impossible to watch, since they are so paranoid that they cause the team to purposely lose them. Other times when the police are sitting on a site they observe other criminal activities such as prostitution, theft, or even drug dealing. Should they get involved or merely ignore the other criminal activity? Sometimes the surveillance team has to disregard other observable crimes that occur before their eyes.

The job of watching Helen and Olga couldn't be considered interesting in that they didn't live the most exciting lives in the criminal world. They trailed Helen to Lizzy's Restaurant, where she often ate by herself and occasionally with friends. However, what was most remarkable was the fact that Helen and Olga never socialized together. It seemed strange that two parties in crime wouldn't eat together or at least meet face to face to discuss their plans. These women had made hundreds of thousands of dollars, but they lived a relatively frugal existence. Olga hung around her old dingy apartment playing her music so everyone in the apartment house could hear her favor classical selections that she enjoyed.

After several days of surveillance, the police noticed that Olga was spending time checking on several elderly gentlemen. Olga's responsibility was to find new homeless victims and provide them a place to stay and food to eat while Helen was like the leader, keeping track of all the life insurance policies. Her accounting system had to be perfect since, if she missed a premium insurance payment, they might lose the coverage on that individual.

On one particular day, Olga spent considerable time with an older man. She met him near the sidewalk and was seen having the man sign documents on the trunk lid of her car. When the officers followed her they saw her take this elderly man to the bank. When they walked out of the bank, Olga had some papers in her hand which she tossed into a trash can. As she drove the man away, the officer approached the trash can and retrieved a bank envelope containing a copy of a document from an insurance company. Later in the day, Olga Rutterschmidt went to an internet cafe and started using one of the computers to try to open a credit card account in someone else's name. Was Olga on the verge of setting up another homeless man for murder?

CHAPTER 13 POLICE HAVE A DILEMMA

The detectives didn't want to arrest the ladies, since the investigation of the case hadn't been completed. The detectives had to continue to check out all the information they had received before thinking about arresting either of them. Prior to their arrests the detectives had only a limited amount of information on the women, but so much still needed to be done. Just like in the infamous O. J. Simpson case, the investigators were caught in a dilemma in that if they arrested someone, they have only 48 hours to file felony charges. If no charges are filed, the person arrested must be released. There is always the fear that if the person is released they may leave the jurisdiction and the police will never be able to bring them to justice.

In the Simpson case, the police put pressure on the DA's Office to file charges before the most incriminating evidence was ever analyzed. When Simpson's attorneys demanded a 'speedy trial', the prosecution was 'in a world of hurt' trying a case before the forensic evidence had been analyzed. In this case, if the women were arrested then charges would need to be filed immediately in order to keep them in custody. The detectives needed more time to develop the case.

However, the LAPD administrators had another way of looking at the case. Since the police had become aware of Olga's activities with the elderly man, the administrators became fearful that these women were about to do another hit-and-run on another victim. The LAPD administration was sensitive to investigations that can turn deadly. Several years earlier, a surveillance team was following two bank robbers who drove to a bank and appeared to be ready to rob the bank. The police didn't want to blow their cover if in fact they weren't going to commit a robbery.

The surveillance officers waited outside, and shortly thereafter the men came out with a hostage and got into the getaway car. The police went into pursuit of the robbers' car. The pursuit lasted several blocks until the robbers' car crashed into an innocent civilian's car. Unfortunately, the hostage and the person driving the other car were killed. The end result was that the civil court held that the LAPD was liable for both deaths since they could have prevented the robbery from happening. The court claimed that the police can't wait on an investigation when innocent lives are involved. Many in law enforcement would disagree with the court's ruling; however, the LAPD administrators didn't want to be sued if in fact the ladies decided in the meantime to run over another homeless man.

Some of the investigators wanted more time to catch the little old ladies red-handed. They believed that they could step in before they attempted to drive over any homeless man. As things stood at that moment in time, the investigators didn't know anything about the car used in the killing. They didn't know anything about the tow truck. The investigators knew they didn't have enough evidence. If they arrested Helen and Olga too early, they could destroy all the records and evidence before the detectives knew what they should be looking for. But the prevailing thinkers in the police administration didn't want to take any chances, so it was decided to obtain search warrants and arrest warrants for both Helen and Olga for the charge of mail fraud. This required the FBI to be involved and the matter would be handled by the U.S. Attorney's Office.

CHAPTER 14 ARREST & SEARCH WARRANT

The U.S. Attorney's Office obtained the arrest warrants for Golay and Rutterschmidt along with search warrants for both of their residences. FBI agents were looking for evidence of life insurance policies and records regarding the maintenance of homeless men. On May 18, 2006, at 7:00 a.m., LAPD and the FBI investigators surrounded Helen's place in Santa Monica near the beach. This was a challenging place to make an arrest since Helen had a six-foot fence surrounding her house. The police would have to pry their way through a very secure gate to get to her front door. There was a large team of officers who surrounded her property. They were able to contact Helen and she was placed under arrest for **Mail Fraud**. She was surprised by the arrest and complained she didn't know anything about Mail Fraud.

When the investigators were able to enter her house, they found shoe box after shoe box with all the information regarding the various insurance policies from numerous companies. Everything was meticulously kept with no chance of forgetting to make a premium payment on time before a policy was terminated. This was a sophisticated operation.

The detectives checked out Helen's Mercedes. In her car they found a Day Planner and the FBI agent looked through it and found a partial license number—FYR482—and a VIN number. The agent took down the numbers to be later checked out. Was that the Mercedes used to run over the victims? The questions were, where the vehicle is and who owned it?

After the police had finished with the search of Helen's place, they were off to Olga's residence in Hollywood. The agents knocked on Olga's third-floor apartment and she answered the door. She was surprised that law enforcement was there to arrest her and search her place. They searched her apartment to see what they could find related to taking care of the homeless men, such as housing and food. They were looking for any receipts or documents showing how they met the homeless at the Hollywood Presbyterian Church. They found eight rubber stamps of signatures which could be used to take out additional policies. The items found included someone else's driver's license, motel and apartment receipts, and numerous suspicious documents.

Later in the day the agents and detectives regrouped to determine what they had found that needed further investigation. One group was assigned to check out all the insurance policies found at Helen's house. Another detective was assigned to track down the killing vehicle to see if that might have been the hit-and-run car. Other detectives had to track down where these homeless men were cared for as far as lodging. Did they have friends and relatives who could show some type of connection between the victims and Helen and Olga?

CHAPTER 15 CONTINUING INVESTIGATION

Since it was decided to make the arrests, everything had to be placed on the 'Fast Track Mode.' However, the search warrants during the arrests uncovered certain items which no one knew how important they were. The shoe boxes full of dozens of life insurance policies found at Helen's place needed to be examined and looked into. The partial vehicle license plate number found in Helen's 'Planner Book' had to be checked out. At Olga's place the finding of the driver's license of Hilary Adams (pseudonym) may or may not have been significant.

Initially, the investigators were trying to find more information about the victims. They had learned that Paul Vados had migrated to the USA from Hungary around the time of the Revolution. He lived with his wife until she died in 1985, after which he moved in and lived with his daughter, Stella. Sometime in 1995, he moved to Northern California, after which Stella lost contact with him. He later returned to the Hollywood area in 1997 and started residing in an apartment on South Fedora Street in Los Angeles.

Further investigation was needed as to the most recent crime scene in the alley behind Westwood Boulevard. The detectives needed to determine if there were any security cameras that could reveal something that might be relevant to the investigation. They decided to review the security cameras in the alley to see what really happened to the victim. The Bristol Farms market was contacted for any video they had of their parking lot and the alley behind their store. The detectives were disappointed that the quality of the tapes was poor and it was hard to make out much of anything. The detectives wondered as to the value of saving such videos, since you can't make out the face of a suspect or even a license plate. The detectives realized that 'beggars can't be choosers' since the companies were voluntarily turning the tapes over to the police.

As poor as the quality of the tapes was, they could provide some information that might prove to be useful. First off, they did see a car at 12:00 midnight that pulled into the alley. They couldn't identify the driver or the license plate number. However, the detectives looked at the lines of the car and thought it looked like a Ford product, either a Taurus or a Mercury Sable. The movement of the car was suspicious as it turned off its lights and after five minutes turned the lights back on.

CHAPTER 16 THE STORY OF THE SABLE

The FBI agent wanted to follow up on the license plate number. The plate number was missing the first digit of FYR482 and the investigator asked if someone could run the VIN number. One of the officers took the VIN number and ran it. He discovered the complete license number was 4FYR482. Next he entered that number in the DMV computer system and it came back to a 1999 Mercury Sable. The police checked to determine who the registered owner was. It turned out that on November 17, 2005, Joe Quin (pseudonym) purchased the Sable at a police impound sale from a Hollywood tow yard. The car had an oil leak, which he repaired. When the DMV history was checked out, it showed that the Sable was impounded for numerous parking violations in Hollywood.

When the detectives received the copies of the citations, they noticed that the car had been parked in several locations only blocks from Olga's apartment. What seemed strange was why the registered owner wouldn't come to the impound lot and pay the fees to reclaim the vehicle. When the detectives looked at the history of the registered owners, they found that an earlier owner of the vehicle was a Hilary Adams. She had listed her address as 823 Croft Avenue, Apt. 18, in Los Angeles.

However, when the detectives ran the name Hilary Adams through DMV, her address was listed on Firmament Avenue, Encino, in the San Fernando Valley.

The detectives made contact with Hilary Adams and she indicated that she had never owned a Mercury Sable and had never lived on Croft Avenue in Los Angeles. At first the detectives were slightly suspicious of this Hilary Adams; however, one of the detectives remembered that **a driver's license with the name Hilary Adams had been found in Olga's apartment**. Special Agent Ted Ochninger, of the FBI, found five photocopies of Adams's driver's license inside an envelope with the notation "Helen sent pictures of: Hilary Adams with an Encino residence address, cell phone number, and birthdate." When the police confronted Hillary Adams about her driver's license, she explained that in April or May of 2003, her purse containing her driver's license and Social Security card was stolen from her locker at the Spectrum Club gym in Santa Monica. She reported it to the police and she had to obtain a new driver's license.

That explained the name of Hilary Adams, but the detectives wanted to check out where was the Sable originally purchased. The DMV records showed that the Sable was sold on January 20, 2004, by Mexicar Auto Sales at 1801 Vermont Avenue, Los Angeles, to a person using the name of Hilary Adams for $6000 in cash. The detectives tracked down the salesman and he remembered the transaction, which involved two older ladies who claimed that they were buying the car for a friend by the name of Hilary Adams. The salesman, Mario Medina, **identified Olga Rutterschmidt as the person who made the purchase** for her friend. The two older ladies wanted the registration to show the address of 823 Croft Avenue for Hilary Adams, even though it was different from the address listed on the driver's license. At that time the car had the license plate number of 4FYR482.

Now the detectives knew about the 1999 Sable, which looked similar to the one seen on the Bristol Farms Market's security camera. They now knew that Olga was involved in the purchase of that Sable by using the name of a person who was on a driver's license found in Olga's apartment. By this time the detectives wanted to inspect the Sable. They went to the new registered owner, Joe Quin, and asked him if they could take his Sable to have it checked out at the police department. Even though it had been months since the death of McDavid, the detectives were hopeful there might be some evidence of the accident. When the detectives started to check out the Sable, they noticed some slight front-end damage. Could that be related to driving over Kenneth McDavid? The police took the Sable to Piper Tech, where the LAPD Crime Lab had a facility to inspect the Sable and examine the undercarriage of the vehicle.

LAPD brought in two CHP accident reconstruction experts. This, however, hadn't been the typical accident where the police were trying to determine the speed of the car or the location of the vehicles involved in an accident. The detectives wanted to see what the CHP experts could find that might connect the car to the killing. They placed the Sable on one of the auto lifts. It was slowly raised up in the air so the CHP experts could walk under it. From underneath they used their flashlights shining on the undercarriage.

The first thing they noticed was there was some slight front-end damage. They moved under the engine compartment and noticed how the undercarriage was so clean. They told the homicide detectives, who were there with them, that older cars tend to drip oil from the engine as well as the transmission areas, causing a coating of oil and grease on the main cross beams of the car. They both remarked how unsoiled the cross beams of the car looked, as though they were wiped clean. The

CHP experts asked the detectives if the victim's clothes were covered in oil. The RHD detective stated that victim McDavid's clothes were covered with caked-on oil stains. It was as if the victim's clothes were used as a rag to wipe the undercarriage off.

The CHP experts then took their flashlights and shined them on the entire undercarriage and started to point to what they claimed was blood and tissue. The RHD detectives called in the Crime Lab CSI crew to start taking swab samples of the various areas pointed out to them. There was no way of knowing for certain which spots should be swabbed, but they tried to take as many samples as possible. They had selected enough spots for testing that it would take the Crime Lab crew several days to analyze them.

Both CHP experts pointed their flashlights to a hose that ran to the bottom of the engine. There was an alligator clamp that was holding the rubber hose to the metal fuel pump line. The two CHP experts started to chuckle to themselves. The RHD detectives asked, "What's so funny?" They both had wide smiles on their face as though they had discovered a nugget. They pointed to the clamp and said, "We know that the Sable hadn't been repaired by a legitimate auto mechanic." They explained that no car agency or garage would use such an alligator clamp since they could lose their State Auto Certification. The detectives looked at each other wondering what the big deal was since the clamp seemed to work perfectly well and it kept the fuel line from leaking.

The detectives weren't going to challenge the Accident Reconstruction experts. They asked them what would happen if that fuel line came disconnected. The CHP guys said that with the Sable you couldn't travel more than a half block before the engine would stop from a lack of fuel. In order to completely understand what the CHP experts meant, the detectives wanted to do a recap to see if they understood what they were saying. If the car ran over a person, that could cause the fuel line to become detached and the car would almost immediately become disabled and be unable to drive.

The CHP experts said that running over a person could easily have pulled off the fuel line. Now the detectives had learned that there was a strong likelihood that the Sable had become disabled. The detectives had two things to follow up on. Was there was some way of knowing if the vehicle was disabled, and could they find out who repaired the vehicle? Was there a mechanic that Helen or Olga might have used to repair the fuel line?

After the inspection of the Sable, the RHD detectives knew that the Sable would have to be confiscated as evidence of a homicide. However, the detectives realized the young couple who had purchased the Sable at the police auction really needed the car since it was their only means of transportation. The police definitively had the power and authority to seize the vehicle. However, the detectives realized that their action was going to mean a totally innocent family would lose their car and not be reimbursed for it. The detectives felt bad in taking the Sable as evidence when the **couple had not been involved in the crime.** In addition, this couple had purchased the auto legally from the police auction.

There are those who wouldn't believe that old time Robbery Homicide detectives would have a heart. However, the detectives somehow worked it out that the Sable was purchased by LAPD. The details were never clear as to whether LAPD purchased the Sable as an undercover vehicle for surveillance purposes. (It would make the perfect undercover car since no crook would suspect any respectable narcotic officer would be seen in this car.) The bottom line was Jose Quin, the new registered owner of the Sable, received his money back that he had paid at the police auction. The

Homicide detectives subsequently were the proud owners of a 1999 Mercury Sable, which was one of the crucial pieces of evidence against Helen and Olga. Years later the Sable was still being used by LAPD; however, no one seemed to remember this was once called the **Killer Car**.

The following graphic page shows the Sable and how it was tracked down.

Graphic 5

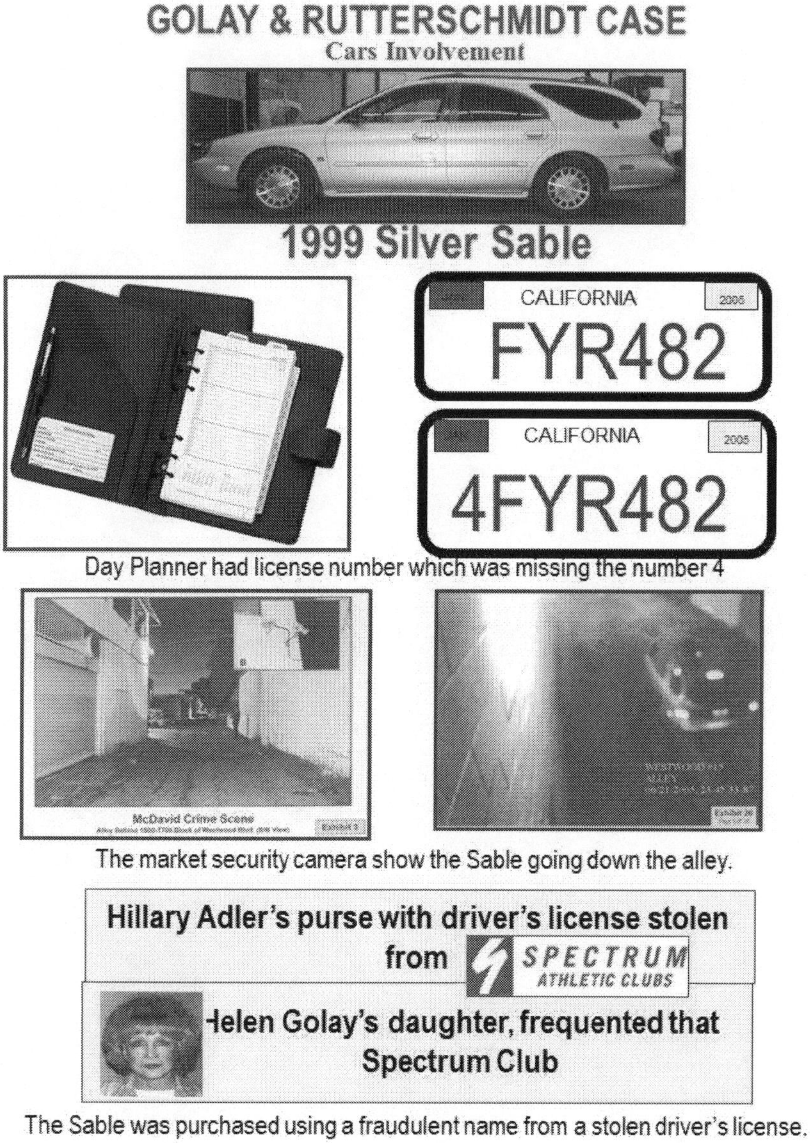
GOLAY & RUTTERSCHMIDT CASE
Cars Involvement
1999 Silver Sable
CALIFORNIA
FYR482
CALIFORNIA
4FYR482
Day Planner had license number which was missing the number 4
McDavid Crime Scene
The market security camera show the Sable going down the alley.
Hillary Adler's purse with driver's license stolen from
SPECTRUM ATHLETIC CLUBS
Helen Golay's daughter, frequented that Spectrum Club
The Sable was purchased using a fraudulent name from a stolen driver's license.

CHAPTER 17 FORENSICS

The detectives had been in contact with the Coroner's Office and they asked them to pull the file on Kenneth McDavid. He had been listed as a male transient who was killed in an alleged hit-and-run. They had analyzed some of his blood to determine his DNA. The detectives needed that result to be sent to the LAPD crime lab. The Coroner's Office sent a copy of his autopsy and toxicology report to the detectives. The report showed that McDavid's blood had a blood alcohol level of .08%. His blood tested positive for a high level of Ambien at .13 micrograms per milliliter of blood, which a person would reach within one or two hours. The result of taking that amount of Ambien would cause a person to fall asleep. There was also a small amount of Hydrocodone (Vicodin) at .09 micrograms and the test also showed positive results for Topamax.

The detectives who were involved with the searching of Helen's house remembered that there was a vial with a powdery substance in it. They didn't confiscate it since it didn't seem to have any relevance at the time. One of the detectives was assigned to obtain another search warrant for Helen's house to retrieve that vial and powdery substances in the bathroom. The vial was recovered and sent to the crime lab for analysis.

The analysis showed the substance in the vial was crushed Ambien. Other pills and substances were found to be Vicodin. The detectives knew now they had the exact drugs found in McDavid's system which were the same as the drugs found in Helen's bathroom. The inference was the substance was used to knock McDavid out in order for the women to be able to drag the unconscious victim from the car into the alley.

The detectives inquired if they were able to obtain a DNA reading from any of the swab samples taken from the undercarriage of the Sable. The lab technician advised the detectives that they obtained several swab samples with the same person's DNA and that they compared it up to the DNA sent by the Coroner's Office. It turned out to be a match of one in ten quadrillion to be that of victim Kenneth McDavid. The detectives shouted out Bingo, which meant that they now had the murder weapon—the Mercury Sable, the so-called 'Killer Car.'

The LAPD investigators in Westside Traffic Division had to feel good, and the LAPD Robbery Homicide Division (RHD) guys realized that it was time to present the evidence to the FBI and the US Attorney's Office. The US Attorney's office on May 19, 2006, charged eight counts of mail fraud. The feds saw a slam dunk case for them, if they prosecuted the case as a Mail Fraud. They might be able to argue for a sentence of 36 to 48 months in a federal country club prison for the elderly federal defendants. LAPD RHD detectives saw these elderly women as murderers, not merely greedy people. There were strong feelings that these women shouldn't be able to get away with murder.

The problem with the murder theory was that no one had seen either woman involved in the death of Paul Vados. He was killed in an alley near La Brea Boulevard, but no one saw what happened, nor was there any forensic evidence to connect them to his tragic death. However, the detectives didn't have any difficulty connecting the women to the killing of McDavid. The homicide detectives felt that the evidence regarding McDavid's death could be used to prove the women were likewise involved in Paul Vados' death.

The following graphic page shows the CSI technician finding dried blood and tissue that matched McDavid's DNA. Below that are photos of how the fuel line was pulled off the fuel pump, causing the car to become disabled.

GOLAY & RUTTERSCHMIDT CASE

Investigation of the Sable

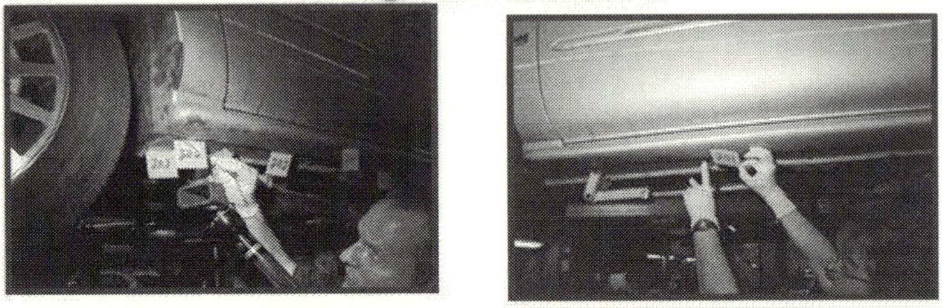

CSI technician taking samples of dried blood and tissue from undercarriage.

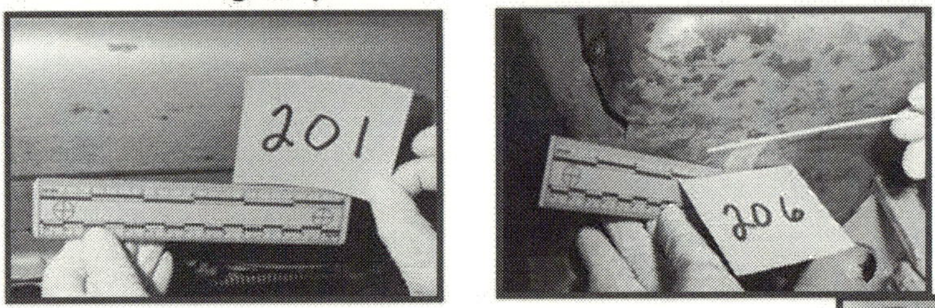

DNA Matched Kenneth McDavid

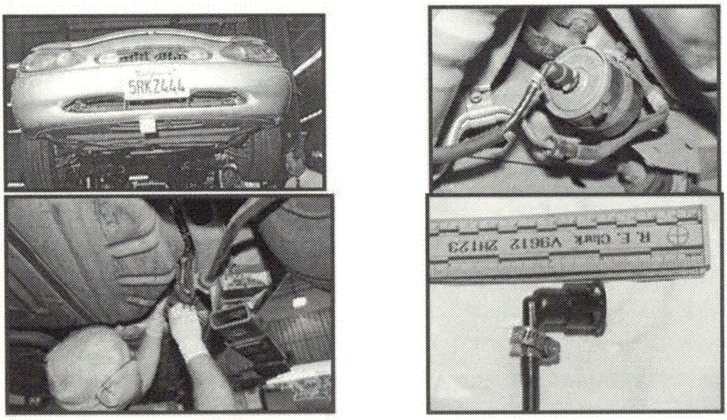

The fuel line became detached from the fuel pump.

Graphic 6

CHAPTER 18 ARRANGING THE INSURANCE POLICIES

How do you obtain life insurance policies for homeless men? Life insurance companies require medical exams, which homeless men wouldn't be able to pass. Helen Golay had learned there were several ways around it. One way was by acquiring **Accidental Death insurance policies**. With those types of policies the insurance companies aren't concerned about the insured's health since they aren't insuring the insured for a natural death. They only pay benefits if the insured is killed by some type of accident. So, homeless men could easily obtain accidental death insurance since the insurance company doesn't care about their personal health.

Besides the Accidental Death Insurance method, a homeless man can get a **Term Life insurance policy** if it is for an extremely low amount. What numerous banks do is provide a new bank account customer with life insurance for $1,000 up to $5,000. Since the amount is so low, the insurance companies don't require a medical examination. The premium rate may be only several dollars a month. Each month the life insurance company sends a premium notice with a form to be filled out if the insured wants to increase the insured amount.

What Helen had learned was that after several months all that had to be done was to check the box and ask the policy be increased to a higher amount, such as $10,000. The insurance company was thrilled that the insured wanted the policy increased, since they would be collecting higher premiums. Since the person already had a policy and had been making payments on time, they never requested a medical exam on such small increases. Then, months later, the insured checked the box to increase the policy limits, this time requesting the policy be increased to $100,000. Even with this higher policy, the insurance company never thought about requesting a medical exam. This can be increased to $500,000 without the insurance company ever requesting a medical exam.

So basically Helen, with the help of Olga, would take the homeless men to banks or other financial institutions and help them fill out the necessary forms and obtain checking accounts. The banks were happy since any new bank account showed an increase in the number of checking accounts. The insurance companies were happy since they had a new insured. The homeless man had to be happy that he truly had a bank account which he could brag to his homeless buddies about.

The women used several methods to make sure the premiums were all paid on time. One way was for Helen to make the payment directly to the insurance company. Another way was to use the homeless man's new bank accounts to pay the insurance premium. In other words, Helen sent a check to the homeless man, who then would deposit it in his new checking account. Subsequently, the homeless person would write the check to the insurance company paying the premiums.

In order to get the bank accounts set up, the women had to obtain basic information from the homeless person. They learned their Social Security number, date and location of birth, and their mother's maiden name. At times there had to be numerous documents to be signed so they had the homeless men clearly write their signature. Olga would take that signature to the local rubber stamp store. There she had a rubber stamp made up as a perfect facsimile of the homeless man's signature. In this way, they didn't have to inconvenience the homeless man every time his signature was needed for some document.

The women screened their candidates for the insurance policies to make sure they didn't have any living relatives who could cause problems by starting to ask questions. It would be disastrous for Helen and Olga if a relative could step in at the last moment and claim to be the true beneficiary of the victim.

Term Life Insurance policies require the existence of an **'Insurable Interest';** that is a relationship between the insured and the beneficiary based on familial, blood, a relationship through marriage, or a financial relationship. The purpose of requiring an 'Insurable Interest' is to prevent a named beneficiary from having the incentive to cause the insured's death.

One of the main concerns of the women was to be listed as the beneficiaries on all the insurance policies. The insurance companies are going to be suspicious if the beneficiaries listed have no ties to the insured. So the women claimed to be either a **cousin or the fiancée** of the homeless man. Listing oneself as a cousin is easy in that it is next to impossible to trace all the cousins that a person might have. It was interesting that Helen played the role of the fiancée, possibly believing no man, even a homeless man, would be interested in an elderly 'Plain Jane' like Olga.

An insurance policy in California becomes **'Incontestable'** after being in force for **two years** as long as the premiums have been paid. Before a policy becomes incontestable, the insurance company can cancel and rescind the policy upon discovery that it was obtained through fraud or misrepresentation. After a two-year period, the policy will remain in force even if it had been procured through deceptive means. A claim that postdates the incontestability period must be paid, unless the insurance company can demonstrate the policy was procured by criminal means.

Insurance companies will typically ask whether the person seeking insurance has other policies on the same insured in order to ensure that the particular insured is not over-insured. In other words, if one of the homeless was killed or died after two years, there would not be an investigation of the claim but merely a direct payment to the beneficiaries. This meant if the women could carry on the charade for two years, they were home free. The only downside was that two years of premiums would amount to thousands of dollars invested in the life of that homeless individual.

The following page shows the lists of the numerous life insurance policies taken out on the homeless victims by the suspects.

Graphic 7

GOLAY & RUTTERSCHMIDT CASE

List of the Life Insurance policies taken out by the suspects for Mr. Vados & Mr. McDavid

Paul Vados Life Insurance Policies

Insur. Co.	Date	Beneficiaries	Relationship Claimed	Amount of Policy	Policy Issued	Money Paid Out
Interstate Assurance	3/27/97	Golay 100%	Golay- Fiancee	$50,000	Yes	Golay- $50,416.79
John Hancock	5/22/97	Golay, Olga Equal	Golay- Fiancee (Cous.) Olga-Cousin	$50,000	No- Info rec from Doc	
Guarantee Trust	10/14/97	Golay 60% Olga 40%	Golay- Fiancee Olga- Cousin	$50,000	Yes	Golay- $30,318.08 Olga- $20,212.06
Monumental Life (Accidental)	10/15/97	Golay, Olga Equal	Golay- Fiancee Olga- Cousin	$187,500	Yes	$192,585 Paid by Court
Hartford CNA (Accidental)	11/1/97	Golay 50% Olga 50%	Golay- Fiancee Olga- Cousin	$150,000	Yes	Golay- $65,875 Olga- $65,875
American Banker's (Accidental)	2/13/99	Golay 50% Olga 50%	Golay- Fiancee Olga- Cousin	$250,000	Yes	Golay- $63,964.39 Olga- $63,964.39
Guarantee (Accidental)	3/1/99	Golay 100%	Golay- Fiancee	$16,000	Yes	Golay- $16,000
Mutual of Omaha (Accidental)	8/4/99					

Kenneth McDavid Life Insurance Policies

Trans-America Life	11/1/02	Golay 100%	Golay- Cousin & Associate	$500,000	No- No Med.	
USAA	11/18/02	Golay 50% Olga 50%		$1,000,000	No- Withdrew	
North American	12/9/02	Golay 100%	Golay- Fiancee	$500,000	No- Withdrew	
Mony 075	1/16/03	Golay 50% Olga 50%	Golay- Invest. Partn. Olga- Invest. Partn.	$500,000	Yes	None- Investigated
AAA Life Insurance	1/17/03	Golay 100%	Golay- Fiancee	$800,000	Yes	Golay- $819,556.3
Mutual of Omaha (Accidental)	2/25/03	Golay 100%	Golay- Nephew & Associate	$14,000 Auto $25,000 Ped.	No- No Paymt	
Globe Insurance	3/7/03	Golay 100%	Golay- Cousin & Associate	$20,000	Yes	Golay- $20,115.75
First Penn Pacific	3/14/03	Golay 50% Olga 50%	G O			

Kenneth McDavid Life Insurance Policies

Garden State Insurance	4/8/03	Golay 100%	Unknown	$100,000	Yes	None- Investigated
Empire General	5/1/03	Golay 50% Olga 50%	Golay- Invest. Partn. Olga- Invest. Partn.	$500,000	Yes	Golay- $251,575 Olga- $251,575
Mony 348	8/6/03	Golay 50% Olga 50%	Unknown	$500,000	Yes	None- Investigated
Globe Life Insurance	8/14/03	Golay 100%	Golay- Fiancee	$20,000	Yes	None- Investigated
United Investor's	10/6/03	Golay 100%	Golay- Fiancee	$100,000	Yes	None- Investigated
Great West Life & Annuity	10/10/03	Golay 100%	Golay- Fiancee	$150,000	Yes	None- Investigated
AARP Life	3/18/04	Golay 100%	Golay- Fiancee	$25,000	Yes	Golay- $75,756
American Life	3/8/05	Golay 100%	Golay- Fiancee & Distant Cousin	$150,000	Yes	None- Investigated

CHAPTER 19 BUILDING A CASE

The detectives thought it would be easy to contact a clearinghouse for the insurance companies to determine how many policies the women had taken out. To the detectives' surprise, there was no such thing as a clearinghouse where all the insurance companies shared their information. What the detectives didn't know was how jealous and possessive the insurance companies were about sharing client information. The competition for insureds is so great that insurance companies don't have a database to check as to how many policies a person may have taken out with other companies.

The detectives asked the insurance companies if they could tell them how many policies listed Helen or Olga as beneficiaries. The insurance companies' response was that policies aren't listed by beneficiary, and besides that, it is highly confidential. When the insurance companies were asked if they check out the insured and beneficiaries on a new policy, the answer was 'No.'

The detectives learned there was no easy way to find out exactly how many dozens of policies the women had taken out for various homeless men over the years. Astonishing as to the practices in the insurance business may seem, the detectives were more interested in running the two names, Paul Vados and Kenneth McDavid. They wanted to know how many policies were set up in those two names.

When checking individually the name **Paul Vados,** the detective found the following insurance companies had issued policies in that name and are listed as follows: Interstate Assurance, John Hancock, Guarantee Trust, Monumental Life (Accidental Life), Hartford CAN (Accidental Life), American Banker's (Accidental Life), Guarantee (Accidental Life), and Mutual of Omaha (Accidental Life).

Under the name of **Kenneth McDavid,** the detectives discovered policies were issued by the following companies: Trans-America Life, USAA, North American, MONY 075, AAA Life Insurance, Mutual of Omaha (Accidental Life) Globe Insurance, First Penn Pacific, Garden State Insurance, Empire General, MONY 348, Globe Life Insurance, United Investor's, Great West Life & Annuity, AARP Life, and American Life.

The women were careful to take out **only one insurance policy per company on each of the victims.** In that way, the insurance companies didn't have any idea that the insured had dozens of policies with other insurance companies.

In order to receive a precise count as to the number of policies, the detectives had to examine all the shoe boxes at Helen's house to find the names of the insurance companies. Since Helen had the premiums all listed according to dates to be paid, the detectives made a list of the names of the insurance companies. Then a detective was assigned to make contact with each insurance company and obtain their records. This included the original application, manner of payment of the premium, and any correspondence regarding that policy.

In Helen's files was the name of the **AAA Life Insurance Company,** each which stood for **the Southern California Automobile Club**. One of the detectives was assigned to contact the Auto Club Life insurance company to obtain all the documents regarding any life insurance policies they had on the victims. The detective explained to the Auto Club representative that the police were suspicious of two elderly women who had taken out dozens of life insurance policies on homeless men in the Los Angeles area. Then the detective explained that the police had discovered information about a car which was used to run over one of the homeless men. The Auto Club staffer became interested in the story. The detective explained that the car may have become disabled after running over the victim. The detective was complaining that they hadn't found the mechanic who fixed the broken fuel line. The staffer was curious and asked when and where the death occurred. The detective said on June 22, 2005, near Westwood and Santa Monica Boulevard.

The Auto Club staffer said that maybe the disabled car might have been towed by the Auto Club Roadside Service. She advised she would check the computer to see if there were any requests for a tow from that location and time. She ran the date through the computer and narrowed the search to tows near Westwood and Santa Monica Boulevards. Within seconds the computer showed there was a **request for a tow for a Mercury Sable by a person by the name of Helen Golay**, who had the car towed to her residence, 1234 Ocean Park Avenue in Santa Ana.

The phone number this person gave was a phone registered to Karen Golay, Helen's daughter. (This phone had been purchased by Karen but used by Helen). The detective couldn't believe his ears. If only the data entry operator hadn't mixed up the spelling of the cities Santa **Ana** for a Santa **Monica** it would have been a bull's-eye. Also, if the cell phone had been registered directly to Helen, then that would have been even better. Now the detectives **could place the disabled Sable near the**

crime scene and **could connect Helen to the Sable** by her use of her Auto Club card to have the Sable towed to her house.

What else did the detectives need to do? They needed to know more about the victims as to how the women controlled them. **Paul Vados** was a homeless man who was 73 years old at the time of his death. He didn't have any close relatives. In other words, at the time of his death no one would come forward to claim his remains. He stayed around the Hollywood Presbyterian Church, which had a Soup Kitchen where he received food and handouts.

The minister of the church remembered Vados and remembered that he appeared to be a perpetual alcoholic who lived on the streets. The minister remembered when Helen Golay and Olga Rutterschmidt came by the church and asked questions about the homeless the church cared for. What was strange about the women was that they wanted information about individual men but showed no interest in volunteering to help serve food at the church.

The women latched on to certain homeless men and tried to provide them a place to stay. First, the women used various motels on Hollywood Boulevard to house these homeless men. The detectives obtained records that showed that the women were paying for weekly stays in the local Econo Lodge.

Eventually, Paul Vados was placed in an apartment where the manager and her 12-year-old daughter kept an eye on him. When the detectives talked to the manager of the complex she indicated that Vados had no job and left in the morning, returning in the evening drunk. At times, they would drop off food for him when he was drunk and couldn't get out for food on his own.

The manager saw Olga come by maybe twice a month to bring him groceries. She had introduced herself as being Paul's sister. He always paid his rent with a money order. Several times Olga was with him when he paid the rent. He didn't have any real friends and no family members he was in contact with. Although he was considered a homeless man, he at least was being cared for by Olga Rutterschmidt. The manager used Olga as the person to contact in case of an emergency. When she didn't see Paul around for several days she contacted Olga. After the accident, Olga came by and told the manager to "dump" all of Paul's belongings, since he had been killed by a bus or a train.

Although Paul Vados was the first of the two to be killed, there was nothing that connected the women with his so-called hit-and-run death. The only information the police had was that the women filed a Missing Person's Report on Vados and later requested a police report on his death. They collected $600,000 in claims on his death as the beneficiary of numerous Life and Accidental Death insurance policies. Det. Willmon had a suspicion as to the manner in which Paul Vados was killed in an alley, but the detectives had no description of the car and no eyewitnesses to the accident.

Kenneth McDavid, who was 50 years old, had a similar background. He grew up in Northern California with his parents and siblings. He attended Sacramento High School and later enrolled at Sacramento State University. He enjoyed music and wanted to be a DJ, so he moved to the Bay area to find jobs. There he demonstrated an interest in screenwriting and came to Hollywood. He joined a list of hundreds of writers who were waiting to be discovered. He had a little success but he couldn't make a living from it. By 1994, he had lost contact with his family and he fell into an alcoholic cycle from which he was never able to find a way out. Eventually, he became a homeless person hanging out near the Hollywood Presbyterian Church.

The women told him that they would provide him a place to stay. In 2002, he took up their offer and moved into the apartment on Cherokee Avenue. This apartment was leased in September 2002, in Golay's name, and she paid the rent by checks on her bank account. He had told one of his roommates that he had signed up for several life insurance policies. He enjoyed living there but he always liked to help other homeless out and permitted others to live with him in the apartment. The women tried to evict the other parties, claiming he could live there only by himself, and the conflict went on for months.

Both Olga and Helen demanded that the manager throw out the other homeless people that lived with McDavid. The women even hired a security guard to stay in the apartment to prevent any homeless people from trying to stay with McDavid. Eventually, a female moved into the apartment and McDavid moved back on the streets. He was a hopeless, homeless alcoholic. Rutterschmidt started paying weekly rent for McDavid to stay in various motels on Sunset Boulevard. This included the Econo Lodge and the Hollywood Studio Inn. Eventually, he returned to the apartment on Cherokee Street.

What was different in the McDavid situation was that Helen took out too many insurance policies and the monthly premiums were becoming too costly. Olga had been against so many policies because she wanted to wait the two years so the insurance companies wouldn't contest the insurance claims. Helen recognized that McDavid would have to be killed before the two-year period. That developed into a major schism between Olga and Helen.

Helen started to try to remove Olga as a beneficiary on some of these extra policies. In this way, Olga wouldn't know about all the extra policies that Helen had taken out. Also, Helen's level of greed may have been the factor for her to try to become the sole beneficiary of many of the accounts. The detectives came across a taped telephone conversation in which Helen called an insurance company and asked that Olga be removed as a beneficiary from the policy. The insurance representative indicated that couldn't be done without Olga's consent. There was a slight rift growing between these two well-seasoned partners in crime over how many policies should be taken out on each victim.

CHAPTER 20 LADIES TALKING

What has made this case so well known in the cyber world is what happened next. Many people have seen on YouTube the famous confrontation between Olga and Helen in the LAPD interview room. The LAPD detectives had dealt with some of the most hardened criminal teams. They had come to the realization that even the toughest conspirators can't help themselves from verbally attacking one another when they are arrested by the police. Always one of them wanted to blame the other for their predicament. The RHD detectives thought maybe it would work between Helen and Olga.

The RHD detectives escorted Helen and Olga into one of the interview rooms in the old Parker Center (prior LAPD Headquarters). After obtaining the basic information from Helen and Olga, the detectives told them they needed a few minutes to check out their stories. The detectives told the woman just to wait in the interview room while they made a few phone calls in the squad room. The detectives walked out, closing the door and leaving the audio-video equipment on.

For a few minutes the women looked at each other without saying a word. Helen Golay hadn't fallen off a turnip truck lately so she remained silent, knowing the room could be wired. Unfortunately for Olga, she couldn't keep her mouth shut any longer. She started to lecture Helen that her greediness had caused the problem. Olga leaned over to where Helen was seated and said, "Helen it's your fault. You can't have that many insurance policies under your name only." Helen warned Olga not to say anything since she thought that the room might be bugged. And Olga tried to contain herself but said, "You did all the extras. You can't do that. You should have had a relationship. This wouldn't have happened."

Helen doesn't know how to shut up Olga. In a sweet, quiet, but firm voice, she explained to Olga that all they had on them was Mail Fraud. She told Olga that there was no evidence of Mail Fraud. She went on to explain that all the insurance companies had joined together in order not to have to pay them. It was interesting that the two women showed righteous indignation. Olga complained that the insurance companies were more than willing to take their money but they weren't willing to pay on the policies. Helen stressed **how unfair** the insurance companies were in not being willing to pay out on the death claims. What was strange about their reasoning was the fact that they had killed the insured in order for them to collect, but their logic seemed to overlook that fact.

For almost five minutes, Olga complained that she couldn't find an attorney to help her sue the insurance companies. She had contacted four attorneys who all claimed that she didn't have a case. Olga asked Helen to share her attorney with her, but Helen was adamant to have an attorney who only represented her.

Olga blamed the insurance company named MONY for starting the investigation. Ed Webster came out to the West Coast to talk to the two of them since they were listed as beneficiaries. If they would have met with him and answered his few questions, these women wouldn't be in the situation they found themselves. Ed

Webster had contacted the other insurance companies, and as a result these companies started reneging on paying out on the policies.

Most people who found themselves in the predicament that Helen and Olga found themselves in wouldn't be thinking of suing the insurance companies. That was exactly what Helen told Olga: "I want to get out of custody and then I am going to sue the MONY insurance company to the gills."

Detective Dennis Kilcoyne came back into the room and asked if they were OK. He said, "Doesn't it feel better to have the handcuffs off?" Both women immediately told him what a bad experience the arrests had been for them. Olga said how embarrassed she was to be in her bare feet and nightgown. She was further outraged that her hair was a mess and she had to walk in front of other neighbors where she had lived for 35 years. She said that it was like a movie nightmare. Dennis advised the women that the FBI agents would be taking them across the street to the federal courthouse.

After Dennis had walked out again, leaving the women alone, Olga couldn't contain herself and told Helen, ***"Why did you take out all the extra policies. That was too many. There is a limit. You were greedy, that was the problem. You fucked up. We had no problems before you got greedy"*** Helen tried to appease Olga and tried to quiet her down. Then Olga blasted Helen one more time by saying, ***"How nice of you to take out the extra ones. They can now go into the others and confiscate them. You didn't listen to me. Big mistake! You are going to jail, honey. They are going to lock you up."***

Helen retained her composure and didn't lose her temper. She used the next few minutes to convey to Olga what she needed to say to the detectives. Helen said, ***"Remember, Kenneth signed for these policies and he wanted us to have them. We***

shouldn't be punished for his action. Remember, Kenneth wanted all of these policies for us even though we don't know why he wanted all this for us."

Helen said, ***"Remember, I was the cousin. You were the fiancée."*** Olga's reply was, ***"Baloney."*** Helen went on to say, ***"I don't know where Kenneth got his money. I gave him some money and you gave him some and we don't know where he got money."*** Then Olga asked the $64,000 question, which was, ***"Why did he give us all those life insurance policies?"*** And Helen calmly replied, ***"He loved us and wanted to be part of our family. We were like his family."***

The question was, how many loving family members drive over other family members in dark alleys? All the planning and hard work both Helen and Olga had done in order to make millions of dollars had all unraveled in the 13 minutes that the two were alone in this police interview room. Later, Helen and Olga thought the police recording of their conversation **JUST WASN'T FAIR.**

The Sheriff is responsible for running the jails, and when they received these two ladies in custody they quickly realized that they had to be housed as 'Keep Aways' from the general population in the jail. This meant that the Sheriff's Department had to transport them to its Lynnwood jail facility. This was a new jail facility for special prisoners. One of their fellow prisoners was Paris Hilton, who was in the cell block one row over. This in a way must have made Helen and Olga feel good that they were housed in the Celebrity section just like Paris Hilton. (During that time period Miss Hilton was serving jail time for Driving Under the Influence).

The following graphic page shows the two suspects alone in the interview room while the recording equipment caught every word they said to each other.

Graphic 8

GOLAY & RUTTERSCHMIDT CASE
Both women left alone in police interview room
Detectives left the recorder on after they left & Olga started to scold Helen for being so greedy.
You did all these insurances extra. That's what raised the suspicion. You can't do that. Stupidity.
No, you're going to go to jail, honey. They are going to lock you up.
The prosecution used the video during the trial

CHAPTER 21 DA'S OFFICE PREPARING THE CASE

When the media saw this case coming, they knew it would create interest and people would want to follow it to see how it turned out. The old saying is 'It ain't news when a dog bites a man, but it is a great story when it is man bites a dog.' The idea of old ladies killing homeless men for life insurance money is the picture-perfect story. It is so contrary to what everyone expects from little old ladies who resemble grandmothers.

Detective Dennis Kilcoyne, one of the senior detectives in the LAPD Robbery Homicide Division, recognized that this case could easily be handled by the U.S. Attorney as a Mail Fraud case. However, that would mean that Helen and Olga would only serve a short time in prison for Mail Fraud crimes. However, if the case were handled right, the DA's Office could put these ladies away for the rest of their lives. Det. Kilcoyne realized it would take a lot of work but there was a good chance the ladies could be convicted of two murders with Special Circumstances (possibly eligible for the Death Penalty).

Det. Kilcoyne had handled some of the most complex homicide cases of all times. He didn't lack experience as to what needed to be done. However, Kilcoyne knew if the Los Angeles County District Attorney's Office were to file murder charges against these elderly ladies, the case would require special attention. He wanted the case to be assigned to the Major Crimes Division headed up by Pat Dixon. At the time, Pat was deeply involved in the Mickey Thompson trial. Kilcoyne knew he needed a top-notch prosecutor on the case. Some of the most experienced prosecutors had publicity cases ready for trial. Deputy D.A. Shelly Samuels had been reassigned to the downtown office from the Van Nuys office and she didn't have a full caseload as of yet. The idea was that she could start the case and eventually try it with Beth Silverman, who was considered one of the best-organized and toughest prosecutors in the high-power unit.

The two prosecutors conducted the preliminary hearing, which resulted in both defendants being held over for trial. However, the preliminary hearing pointed up some deficiencies in the case. The problem with trying the case was that it was made up of hundreds of documents. When someone explained the case, they said that the women took out dozens of life insurance policies on these two homeless men. The problem at trial was that each and every policy had to be proved to the jurors by using documents (Boring Boring). The monotonous reference to dozens of insurance policies would cause the jurors to lose interest in the case.

Det. Kilcoyne recognized that a prosecutor needed a way to explain the case to jurors without getting lost in all the weeds. Beth Silverman was the perfect prosecutor since she had a way of communicating with jurors without becoming tangled up in all the details. Considerable work was done on the case by Beth until she was sent out for trial on a mammoth case that would tie her up for the next year.

In the meantime, the other prosecutor, Shelly Samuels, was transferred to another assignment.

All of a sudden, Det. Kilcoyne realized that the Golay and Rutterschmidt case was floating along without a captain and the trial date was nearing. In May of 2007, Bobby Grace and Truc Do had prosecuted Chester Turner, the most prolific serial rape/murderer of all times. These prosecutors not only received convictions but convinced the jury to recommend the Death Penalty for defendant Chester Turner. So, all of a sudden there was a dynamic duo who were unstoppable. Det. Kilcoyne went to the DA administration and asked for the best of the best prosecutors for the Golay/Rutterschmidt case. It was a no-brainer that Bobby Grace and Truc Do had a winning track record. Bobby had some high-powered cases that had to be continued, which was worked out. That meant that Bobby and Truc were available to take on the so-called 'Black Widow' case.

The two prosecutors didn't have any time to rest and were immediately meeting with Det. Kilcoyne to get a crash course as to the facts of the Golay/Rutterschmidt case. Bobby Grace had a reputation for utilizing PowerPoint presentations since he had learned how that it was the most effective way to keep the jurors' attention, especially in complex cases like this one with hundreds of critical documents.

No one could ignore the two-ton elephant in the room. That described the fact that the two defendants projected a **sympathetic appearance**. Every juror would initially feel compassion for the two elderly ladies. Everyone's reaction was the two ladies didn't look like criminals or act like criminals. Initially there was a feeling that there has to be an explanation for their conduct. Maybe one of them was dying of cancer and needed money to save her life. Or, maybe they were blackmailed to commit the crime. Possibly they had been poorly treated by an insurance company and just wanted to strike back at the insurance industry to teach them a lesson.

The prosecutors realized that they would have to be more than convincing. This was the type of case that would require the prosecutors to prove their case by 150%. The prosecutors could say this is an unfair burden on them, but the answer is to know how to go about presenting the evidence and to be overwhelmingly persuasive. In other words, you need to make sure that you don't lose any of the jurors when you are trying to prove someone's guilt.

(The author was brought in early on to assist in the creation of the most effective way to present the facts to jurors. The author will explain the presentation he prepared for use in the trial.) Initially, the prosecution needed to have a slide or chart that showed the Relationship of the Parties. The first slide showed two photos with the names of the two defendants on top and underneath the photos of the victims with their names. This is often referred to as 'Who's Who in the Zoo.'

The prosecutor needs to spend some time at the beginning introducing the jurors to the parties so they have time to absorb this critical information. If the jurors don't have this firmly embedded in their mind, they won't be able to follow the various descriptions of what happened to whom. The idea they wanted to convey to the jurors was that there were two separate incidents: those facts that pertain to Paul Vados's death and the facts that involved McDavid's death.

Next, the prosecutors needed a way to explain the scam the women were utilizing. The prosecutors didn't want to go into too much detail but just enough so the jurors understood how the women were able to get so many insurance policies. The jurors needed to understand the difference between **Term Life Insurance** vs. **Accidental Death Insurance**. Everyone at some time in their life has had to listen to an insurance agent try to explain to them the difference between these types of life insurance plans. It is crucial to know what is the appropriate type of insurance one needs for the security of one's family. Therefore one tries to understand all the differences and what the variables and risks are.

Talking about life insurance is one of those topics that can result in a person having a glazed look like, "I don't know what the hell you're talking about, but I will be polite and not interrupt you." So the prosecutors recognized the challenge and went to work in simplifying what the jurors needed to know about the insurance business. All that information was incorporated in a slide that graphically showed what the prosecutors were talking about.

Similarly, the jury needed to comprehend the relevant information from so many insurance policies. There were over 40 insurance policies, and each one was slightly different from the others. The secret was to place all the policies on one slide, which gave the jurors a comfort level that it wasn't too complex to understand. They could see it all fit on one page. The idea was to group the policies by the name of each victim. The chart had to include the insurance company's name, date, amount, beneficiaries, relationship of beneficiary, and money paid out. That is a lot of data on a chart, but it was all readable. The prosecutors listed all **eight** of Paul Vados' insurance policies on one page. It worked well and made it much easier to see all the policies as to Vados. *The next graphic page shows this chart.*

Graphic 9

Paul Vados Life Insurance Policies

Insur. Co.	Date	Beneficiaries	Relationship Claimed	Amount of Policy	Policy Issued	Money Paid Out
Interstate Assurance	3/27/97	Golay 100%	Golay- Fiancee	$50,000	Yes	Golay- $50,416.79
John Hancock	5/22/97	Golay, Olga Equal	Golay- Fiancee (Cousin.) Olga-Cousin	$50,000	No- Info rec from Doc	
Guarantee Trust	10/14/97	Golay 60% Olga 40%	Golay- Fiancee Olga- Cousin	$50,000	Yes	Golay- $30,318.08 Olga- $20,212.06
Monumental Life (Accidental)	10/15/97	Golay, Olga Equal	Golay- Fiancee Olga- Cousin	$187,500	Yes	$192,585 Paid by Court
Hartford CNA (Accidental)	11/1/97	Golay 50% Olga 50%	Golay- Fiancee Olga- Cousin	$150,000	Yes	Golay- $65,875 Olga- $65,875
American Banker's (Accidental)	2/13/99	Golay 50% Olga 50%	Golay- Fiancee Olga- Cousin	$250,000	Yes	Golay- $63,964.39 Olga- $63,964.39
Guarantee (Accidental)	3/1/99	Golay 100%	Golay- Fiancee	$16,000	Yes	Golay- $16,000
Mutual of Omaha (Accidental)	8/4/99	Golay 100%	Golay- Fiancee	$25,000	Yes	Golay- $25,000

However, the prosecutors couldn't use this concept in the McDavid case since there were **30** policies, with so much data that it couldn't all fit on one page. Years ago the author was taught by his boss that anything worth writing about had to fit on one page. This boss had been in the Marine Corp. and he said, "The job of the subordinate was to place everything important on one page." In the old M*A*S*H TV series, it was the character named "Radar O'Reilly" who was the assistant to Colonel Sherman T. Potter. Radar prided himself in putting all the orders he wanted carried out on one page. There had been numerous studies that showed that top executives will read and comprehend what is listed on the first page. Seldom does a busy executive make it to the second or following pages. Part of the reasoning is that many executives believe what is listed on the subsequent pages isn't as pressing and doesn't require immediate attention.

Remembering the 'One Page' concept, the author tried hard to list all of Kenneth McDavid's insurance policies on one page. Since there were 30 insurance policies, when the author listed them on one page the print and font size was so small it couldn't be read. Squeezing it all on the one page made it look like the bottom line of an optometrist's eye exam chart.

It became obvious that Helen Golay had taken out so many policies on Kenneth McDavid that they couldn't possibly fit on one page. So it was decided to use two slides and the prosecutor could explain that there were so many policies you can see that they can't be listed on one chart. By doing this, the jurors could sense the unbelievable number of policies that had been taken out on McDavid.

The prepared PowerPoint included several maps that showed the jurors where the various events took place. One map covered all the area from Santa Monica where Helen lived to the Hollywood area, where Olga rented an apartment and the homeless men were housed. There also was a more detailed map of the various alleys where the homeless men were run down, as well as where the car was disabled and had to be towed.

The prosecutors knew that the jurors would have difficulty figuring out the McDavid crime scene, so LAPD put up a helicopter to take several aerial photos that showed the alley and how it extends to the Chevron service station. They used this as an exhibit to make it crystal clear where the security camera showed the Sable vehicle entering the alley.

They took a few of the insurance applications and enlarged them. Then they highlighted the important information such as date, amount, and beneficiaries. This way the prosecutors in their Opening Statement could go through an application and the various data that must be included. They did the same with a claim form showing all the items that the women had to include in order to make a claim and get paid.

The prosecutors had several exhibits made up that included the relevant photos of each crime scene, showing the position of the victim's body in the alley. They did the same as to the search of the undercarriage of the Sable, showing exactly where they found the blood and tissue that they had analyzed to compare to McDavid's DNA.

In other words, the prosecutors weren't going to take a chance that a juror might become lost in the myriad of details and all the hundreds of documents. Bobby Grace and Truc Do were masters of using PowerPoint to educate the jurors as to the facts of the case and to see how all the facts interrelated to each other. Many speakers say it is just a matter of connecting the dots. So in the short time the prosecutors had to prepare, they did their best to figure out the best way to present the evidence to the jurors. Their mission was to focus the jurors' attention on what these old ladies did and let the Defense deflect the attention from the facts to generating sympathy for these two senior citizen defendants.

CHAPTER 22 READY FOR TRIAL

The DA's Office Death Penalty Committee (technically called the Special Circumstances Committee) had to decide whether to seek the Death Penalty on either of the defendants. It was hard for anyone on the Committee to think of a case with a **greater degree of Premeditation**. As to the deaths of Paul Vados and Kenneth McDavid, the women housed and fed them knowing all the time that they were going to kill them in the most horrific way. Opponents of the Death Penalty are extremely concerned that the people executed do not feel any pain during the execution process. In order to carry out an execution, the States have been required to create a concoction of various drugs to make sure that the vicious killers do not suffer any discomfort during their execution.

However, can you imagine the pain and discomfort Paul Vados and Kenneth McDavid felt when the car tires crushed their rib cage and squashed all their organs? Their brains would continue to function for a period of time, possibly causing the most excruciating pain until death finally ended their agony. As one of the detectives suggested, it was like the two women were fattening up the turkeys until the critical day when they have to chop their heads off.

The premeditation factor had to weigh heavily on the Committee members. However, from the practical side, even if they were able to obtain the Death Penalty there was no way these defendants would live long enough for it to be imposed. Also, neither of them had any type of criminal record, even though they had been scamming people for years. It would seem that the mitigating factors, as to both of them, would outweigh the high level of Premeditation exhibited in this case.

Many speculated that if the DA agreed to a plea bargain the women would be willing to receive Life without Possibility of Parole for dropping the Death Penalty. However, the Los Angeles County DA's Office has a policy against such a settlement. Philosophically, the DA's Office believes that bargaining with the Death Penalty isn't a good policy. Only in extraordinary circumstances will the DA's Office permit a Death Penalty to be reduced for a plea of guilty for **L**ife **W**ith **O**ut the possibility of **P**arole (LWOP).

On October 24, 2007, the DA's Office announced that it wouldn't seek the Death Penalty on either defendant. This was a signal that the case would have to go to trial, which it did on March 18, 2008. The jury was made up of nine men and three women, and the trial was expected to last three months. It was agreed that the case would be tried before Judge David Wesley. He was the Supervising Judge for the Criminal Courts Building and was a knowledgeable and a practical judge in handling his court calendar.

The defendants' appearance at time of trial was less flashy than when they made their first court appearance. They looked their age, and now Helen was 77 and Olga was 75. They were in their pantsuits and their long gray hair was straight due to a lack of rollers and hair spray, which they had requested but were denied.

CHAPTER 23 TRIAL

The prosecutor, Truc Do, made the Opening Statement. She said, "They started this murder plot with greed, and you're going to see that even when the jig was up these defendants remained greedy. They waited for two years with murder on their mind." She took the jurors through the facts by using a PowerPoint presentation and explained what witnesses would be testifying to. She waited to the end of her Opening when she played the police video of Rutterschmidt complaining to Helen that it was her fault for taking out too many policies.

The lengthy trial began with **Special Agent Robert Brockway** of the California Department of Insurance, who testified as an expert in insurance matters. He laid the foundation for the jurors to understand the insurance business procedures.

Detective Willmon testified that he investigated the incident of Paul Vados' death on November 8, 1999, in the alley at 307 North La Brea. He assumed it was a fatal traffic accident. When he arrived at the dark alley it was raining heavily. The victim's body was lying cross-wise in the middle of the alley. He had no wallet and no identification on his person. It appeared that he had been lying on the ground when he was struck by a car. His chest and torso were twisted and crushed. His injuries and the placement of his body indicated that he had been run over by a car traveling slowly. There were no glass fragments or any car parts at the scene.

Officer William Fernandez testified that he took a missing person report from the defendants on November 17, 1999, at the Wilshire Police Station. They claimed to be relatives and had checked on his place finding no one home, except for a TV which was playing.

Det. Willmon testified that Helen Golay called him on December 3, 1999, and said that she was a one-time fiancée and wanted an accident report. He couldn't provide her with a report since she was not a relative; however, Rutterschmidt, who claimed to be a cousin, was able to obtain the police report. The next witness up for the prosecution was **Dr. Louis Pena**, a forensic pathologist who conducted Paul Vados' autopsy. He testified that the victim was 73 years old and he died as a result of multiple traumatic injuries, including 48 fractures to his ribs. The trauma to the victim caused a fatal laceration to his aorta. In Paul Vados' autopsy, the medical examiner was unable to find any broken legs. Also, his clothing was covered in grease. His opinion was the injuries were consistent with having been run over by a car.

The prosecutors had to call **each insurance company** and have them testify to the issuance of their policy. An example of their testimony was as to the one for **Continental Casualty Insurance Company** that issued a $250,000 Accidental Death Insurance policy on Vados' life. The beneficiaries were Olga as his cousin and Helen as his fiancée. The latter made the premium payment and submitted the claim for death benefits. Helen and Olga received $65,875 each.

Another witness testified for **American Bankers,** which had issued a $250,000 life insurance policy on Vados, with his residence given as Golay's address and both defendants were the beneficiaries. Helen made the premium payments from a bank account in Vados' name, but under Helen's address and phone number. Each defendant was paid $63,974 in death benefits.

Minister Charles testified that he worked at Hollywood Presbyterian Church and met the women, who wanted to know about homeless men. He showed the two around and explained that many of the homeless live around the church. After he showed them all the services that the church provided, he thought they would want to volunteer to help, but they didn't.

Considerable testimony came from a **Patrick Lane** (pseudonym), who was a homeless person from Michigan. He referred to himself as being an urban camper. He explained to the jury that he had gotten to know Kenneth McDavid, who was very fortunate in that these elderly ladies leased a nice apartment on Cherokee Street that he could call home. Kenneth liked to help out those who hadn't been as fortunate as he had been. Kenneth permitted Lane to stay with him in the apartment. On numerous occasions both Olga and Helen came by demanding that Lane and his girlfriend move out.

Lane complied and moved out but eventually moved back in. Olga hired an armed guard to stay in the apartment and not let anyone else stay there except for McDavid. Lane testified that the problem resulted in Helen withdrawing her lease and McDavid then started living week by week in various motels on Sunset Boulevard. The women paid cash to have a place for McDavid to stay.

The next testimony involved the ownership of the Sable, starting with the salesman, **Marion Medina,** who sold the Sable to Olga in the name of Hilary Adams. Next, **Mrs. Adams** testified to having her wallet stolen at the Spectrum gym and having her driver's license taken. She said she didn't know the defendants and never purchased or directed anyone to purchase the Sable.

To complete the circle of the Sable, FBI agent **Ted Oehninger** testified how and where he found the envelope in Olga's apartment that contained Hilary Alder's driver's license. Additional witnesses testified to writing parking tickets on the Sable as it was parked on the streets near Olga's place. It all ended with the testimony of **Jose Quin** (pseudonym), who was the lucky or unlucky soul who bought the Sable at a police auction.

Officer Michael McGann testified he was the first officer on the scene involving McDavid. He didn't see any abrasions; however, there were tire marks on the victim's clothing. On the ground in the alley there were no skid marks, no pieces of glass, or parts from the car.

Detective Hernandez testified he responded to the incident that occurred on June 22, 2005, after midnight in the alley behind Westwood Boulevard and noticed that the victim still had his glasses on. He could see the victim's chest was flattened and a tire imprint on his jeans.

Witnesses for the Bristol Farms Market testified to video from their security camera showing a car entering the alley and turning off the auto lights for five minutes, then turning them back on and reappearing. The detectives had reviewed the tapes and believe the vehicle to be an SUV Sable or Taurus.

Det. Hernandez found no eyewitnesses and listed it as a possible hit-and-run. Later in August Olga Rutterschmidt came to the station and asked for a police report, claiming to be a cousin of McDavid. She showed no emotions about the loss of this relative.

Deputy Medical Examiner Solomon Riley concluded that McDavid's death was caused by multiple blunt force trauma to his upper body. The Coroner found that he had no broken legs but he had a flattened chest and three broken ribs, fractured spine, abrasions, and the body had been dragged. Next from the Coroner's Office was **Joseph Muto**, a toxicologist and a certified blood-alcohol analyst. He was the laboratory director for the Coroner's Office, and four laboratory analysts worked under this witness.

Crime lab representative Muto testified that Kenneth McDavid had a blood alcohol level of .08% and traces of Ambien, Vicodin, venlafaxine, and temazepam were found in his system.

Muto testified that his analysts had the data generated by their equipment to the clerical staff, who prepared a report reflecting the test results, which was peer reviewed and then made into a final report which he testified from. Muto then signed off on the report indicating that he found that the analysis was done in the normal course of business and was accurate. The judge allowed him to testify as to the result of the toxicology report even though he was not the one who conducted the test. (This became the sole legal issue raised on appeal).

Cheryl Will, supervisor for the crime lab, found blood and human tissue in eight spots on the undercarriage of the Sable. She had those items analyzed for DNA and they matched Kenneth McDavid's DNA.

A **witness from the Auto Club** testified that she was contacted about her company issuing a life insurance policy in the name of Kenneth McDavid. The detective told her about the possibility that the car had broken down. She checked to see if any requests for towing were made. She entered into her computer the approximate time and the general location and it showed that a party by the name of Helen Golay had requested towing services at 11:51 p.m. from the Chevron service station two blocks from the crime scene.

The **tow truck operator, Luis Jaimes**, from Brent-Air Towing, responded and towed a Mercury Sable to Golay's residence in Santa Monica. He couldn't identify who the person was, but he remembered she was an older female. There was brief testimony that the fuel line had been disconnected. Later, someone reconnected the fuel line with an alligator clamp, which was not the proper method of fixing fuel lines.

As a side issue, the prosecution called **Joey Reynolds** (pseudonym), who worked for the insurance company, to testify that he received a telephone call from Olga Rutterschmidt claiming that she was concerned about some type of insurance fraud since she was really the victim's fiancée. On June 5, 2005, he received a call from Helen Golay wanting to remove Rutterschmidt as co-beneficiary from the policy. He told her that couldn't be done without the insured agreeing to it. Only two weeks later, McDavid was dead and a claim was submitted.

The prosecution then called **Jimmy Collins** (pseudonym), who testified how the women used homeless men. He explained that Olga came up to him at Burger King and told him that she could provide him a place to live. Since he was broke and living on the streets, he agreed to accept the help from Olga and another woman named Helen. All he had to do was supply them with some basic information about himself. It wasn't long before they had taken out an $800,000 insurance policy on his life. Olga was continuing to want more and more personal information about him. Jimmy didn't feel that things were right, and he ran away from them. Jimmy's intuition of bad vibes saved him from becoming the women's next victim.

A life insurance expert testified that there were a total of 12 life insurance policies taken out on Paul Vados. The insurance companies paid out to the two women $2,200,000.

As to Kenneth McDavid, there were 13 insurance policies for a total of $3,700,000. At the time of the arrests, Helen Golay had received $2,540,767 and Olga Rutterschmidt had received $674,571. The women were in the process of suing for the remainder that the insurance companies had not paid.

The most dramatic part of the testimony came from **Detective Dennis Kilcoyne**, who was the lead detective from the Robbery Homicide Division. He testified that after the defendants had been arrested they were brought to Parker Center. He placed the two ladies in the same room at the police station and surreptitiously videotape recorded them. He had told them that they were charged with mail fraud and were under investigation for murder. He left the room claiming he had to make several phone calls in order to get them transferred to the federal authorities. At that point, the prosecution played for the jury the video of the two women going after each other verbally at the police headquarters.

CHAPTER 24
INCREDIBLE DEFENSE

On March 20, 2008, a tow truck with a car attached negotiated its way into the basement of the Criminal Courts Building (CCB). The tow operator slowly dropped the vehicle to the concrete floor. How could such an unattractive Sable vehicle receive so much attention? Later in the day, the jury was escorted to an exclusive showing of the infamous 'Killer Car.' The jurors were given a chance to walk around the vehicle and poke their heads next to the glass windows to get a view of the interior of the car.

Even other judges in the CCB came down to get a look at the old ladies 'Killer Car.' This was like a big cattle auction and everyone was uncertain what they should be looking for or at. The biggest concern was the jurors leaning over to see how this car could run over a human being. The judge then asked the jurors if they had seen enough and told them to congregate over by the elevator to return to the courtroom. The tow truck returned and picked up the infamous Sable and drove it back to Piper Tech, the police storage area where it was again parked. (Apparently everyone forgot about the poor old Sable and it stayed parked in the police yard for years, no one knowing what to do with it.)

Helen's attorney, Roger Diamond, was a well-known attorney in the LA Courts. His claim to fame was that he had represented many defendants who were involved in the pornography business. He loved to talk about the First Amendment and how important it was that everyone has the right to Free Speech. Roger felt that no matter how obscene an act or photo might appear, a pornographer had rights. He was adamant that the founding fathers meant to protect pornography. Consequently, any photograph of the most erotic act imaginable had the same rights to be viewed by the public just like the Mona Lisa.

Everyone wondered why Helen selected Roger Diamond from the thousands of attorneys in Los Angeles. When the media cornered Roger, he always claimed that his client had an explanation for everything. Helen and Roger didn't appear to have much in common.

When it came time for the Opening Statements, Diamond said he would reserve his Opening until after the prosecution had presented all their evidence. After the DA had finished presenting their evidence, the judge asked Roger if he wanted to make an Opening Statement on behalf of his client; he replied that he did. He said, "Helen Golay is a little old lady who couldn't have done what she is charged with and allegedly did in this case. It was Karen Golay, her daughter, who is in the physical condition capable of pulling a body out of a car to lay it in an alley and run over it." **No one saw this Defense coming**. All of a sudden Helen's attorney was telling a tall tale that it was Helen's daughter who had collaborated together with Olga to commit these crimes.

Her attorney told the jury that he was going to call all these witnesses to prove it was a joint venture between Karen and Olga. The prosecution objected since these witnesses names hadn't been turned over in pretrial Discovery. The judge agreed that they couldn't be called. The defense attorney stated he would rely on his cross-examination of the prosecution witnesses to prove his case. Diamond went on to explain that Helen's daughter disliked her mother, who didn't approve of Karen's boyfriend. He claimed that Karen had used Helen's auto club card to have the Sable towed. Also, it was Karen's phone that was used to contact the dealership where the Sable was purchased. Furthermore, Karen was a member of the Spectrum Gym Club where the wallet and identification of Hilary Adams had been stolen.

This, without a doubt, was a peculiar Defense, especially since it appeared that Helen wasn't going to testify. The question on everyone's mind was, how could Helen and her attorney possibly put on such a Defense?

Olga's Public Defender had to have been taken by surprise with Helen's Defense. He stated that Helen Golay had manipulated the simple-minded Rutterschmidt to do certain things to take care of the homeless men. He explained that Olga may be guilty of fraud but she had nothing to do with the deaths of the victims. The Public Defender indicated that they weren't going to put on any witnesses but maintained that the prosecution hadn't proved its case of murder beyond a reasonable doubt.

CHAPTER 25 HOW IT ALL ENDED

The prosecution argued that the two elderly ladies were the worst of the worst. He claimed, "They didn't need this money. They weren't poor and destitute." He argued they went out of their way to target men who had nothing.

The Ladies' Plan was to recruit homeless men by offering them free room and board. Once the victims agreed, the women convinced the men to sign documents or forged their signatures on insurance applications. The defendants isolated the victims from their family and friends and they closely kept track of the movement of the victims.

The manner in which the defendants carried out the Plan enabled them to obtain the insurance policies by applying for Term Life Insurance and Accidental Death Insurances. The defendants were involved in elaborate phony insurance verifications. After the insurable waiting periods had been satisfied, the elderly ladies killed the men all by themselves. They did this by staging hit-and-run accidents. The defendants arranged to claim the bodies of the victims by deceitfully claiming to be a family member.

The case was broken by a combination of various LAPD detectives and a suspicious insurance fraud investigator who noted the fact that Golay and Rutterschmidt were beneficiaries on numerous policies.

Helen's attorney vigorously argued, "This is a travesty of Justice. It's unfortunate that two men are dead. But she didn't do it."

The Public Defender argued to the jury that it was Helen Golay who was the brains behind the operation. He explained that it was Helen who was trying to have Olga eliminated as one of the beneficiaries on the various policies. He said, "Is it reasonable to believe that Helen Golay would dupe and double-cross Olga Rutterschmidt, who had evidence and knowledge that Helen Golay killed Mr. McDavid?"

The prosecutor, Bobby Grace, utilized his Rebuttal Argument to address the claims by Helen's attorney that her daughter, Karen Golay, was the real person behind the killings. Bobbie showed that Karen would not gain one dime from either Paul Vados or Kenneth McDavid's death. She was not listed as the primary beneficiary upon either of the victims' deaths. Helen and Olga were the only ones who would be able to make a claim for the insurance money. Therefore, Karen had no motive to harm the victims.

Prosecutor Grace forcefully responded to Olga's attorney's Argument that she was too simple-minded and was kept in the dark as to the killings. He said they were partners and equally worked for equal split. Olga was the main person who looked after the victims. The Defense had stated that Olga had shown some compassion for Paul Vados. The prosecutor stated Olga's concern for victim Vados was no more than the fact she wanted to keep him alive so they could collect on their investment.

The major point made by Olga's attorney in his Argument was that Olga was a mere follower and the leadership role was played by Helen. However, the video of the defendants talking to each other at the police headquarters showed that Olga wasn't afraid to stand up to Helen and even taking her on for being too greedy.

When the prosecution finished their Rebuttal Argument, Judge Wesley proceeded to read the Jury Instructions. Most of the Instructions were the standard ones, since there was no reason to give lesser offenses such as Manslaughter. Second-degree Murder also didn't have to be considered. If you believed the prosecutor's evidence, this case could only be described as Premeditated First Degree Murder.

The trial lasted five weeks and deliberations had taken longer than anticipated. On April 18, 2008, after one week of deliberation, the jury came back with a guilty verdict as to Helen Golay for two counts of First Degree Murder and one for Conspiracy to Commit Murder.

It was interesting that the jury had deadlocked as to Olga Rutterschmidt. Apparently, the Public Defender's Argument that Olga was too simple of a person and that she couldn't be guilty of murder had had some impact on the jurors. The judge agreed to excuse a juror who had a trip planned and an alternate was called to replace the excused juror. The judge even discussed the possibility of allowing the prosecutor and public defender to reargue the case, but at the last minute rejected that idea. Now with this new juror the jury had to restart their deliberation. Eventually, the jury came back with a guilty verdict as to Olga for two counts of First Degree Murder and one count of Conspiracy to Murder.

As to both women, the jury found the Special Circumstances true for multiple murders and financial gain, which meant that neither defendant could be released on parole.

At the time of sentencing, several of the victims' relatives had been located. They came in to address the court that the victims might have been homeless at the time of their deaths but they had been mentally and physically productive members of society before alcoholism took over their lives.

Kenneth McDavid's sister, Sandra Salman, claimed that Kenneth was a lover of music and had high hopes when he graduated from Cal State Sacramento. Music was his main love in life, which led him to San Francisco where he worked as a DJ. He had dreamed of being a screenwriter in Hollywood; however, that hope for success didn't materialize.

Paul Vados' daughter, Stella, came to court and related how her dad had for years led a productive life.

Jimmy Collins, who was 48 years old, was the next in line to be a victim. He related how Olga had approached him at the Burger King and promised him shelter. He was desperate and appreciated the help. However, Olga continued to demand personal information from him. They were able to obtain a life insurance policy in his name for $800,000. He became suspicious and one day he walked away from them. His good instincts most likely saved his life.

At the end of the sentencing hearing, Judge David Wesley said, "**THESE UNFORTUNATE MEN WERE SACRIFICED ON YOUR ALTAR OF GREED**." He sentenced both Helen and Olga to Life Without the Possibility of Parole (LWOP).

The following graphic page was used by LAPD in their Homicide Exhibit of notorious cases that they had investigated.

Graphic 10

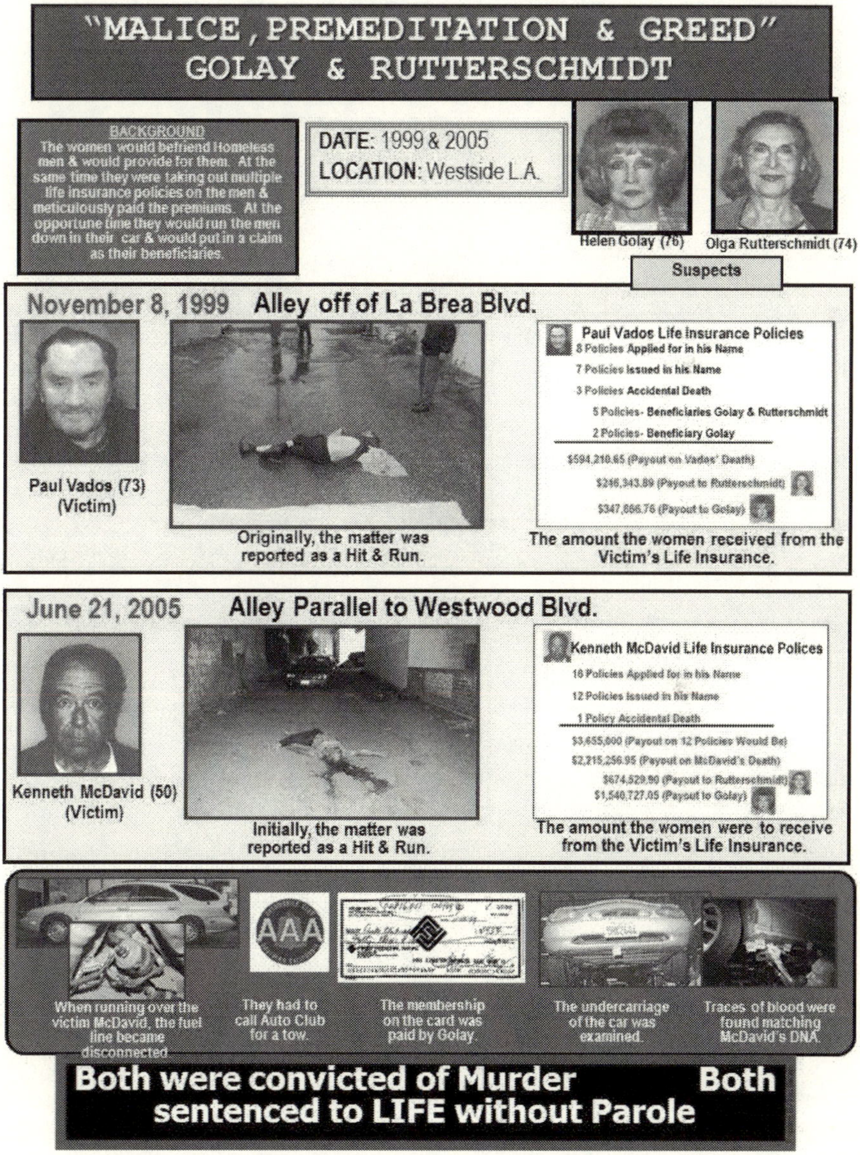
"MALICE, PREMEDITATION & GREED"
GOLAY & RUTTERSCHMIDT
BACKGROUND
The women would befriend Homeless men & would provide for them. At the same time they were taking out multiple life insurance policies on the men & meticulously paid the premiums. At the opportune time they would run the men down in their car & would put in a claim as their beneficiaries.
DATE: 1999 & 2005
LOCATION: Westside L.A.
Helen Golay (76)
Olga Rutterschmidt (74)
Suspects
November 8, 1999
Alley off of La Brea Blvd.
Paul Vados (73)
(Victim)
Originally, the matter was reported as a Hit & Run.
Paul Vados Life Insurance Policies
8 Policies Applied for in his Name
7 Policies Issued in his Name
3 Policies Accidental Death
5 Policies- Beneficiaries Golay & Rutterschmidt
2 Policies- Beneficiary Golay
$594,210.65 (Payout on Vados' Death)
$246,343.89 (Payout to Rutterschmidt)
$347,866.76 (Payout to Golay)
The amount the women received from the Victim's Life Insurance.
June 21, 2005
Alley Parallel to Westwood Blvd.
Kenneth McDavid (50)
(Victim)
Initially, the matter was reported as a Hit & Run.
Kenneth McDavid Life Insurance Polices
16 Policies Applied for in his Name
12 Policies Issued in his Name
1 Policy Accidental Death
$3,655,000 (Payout on 12 Policies Would Be)
$2,215,256.95 (Payout on McDavid's Death)
$674,529.90 (Payout to Rutterschmidt)
$1,540,727.05 (Payout to Golay)
The amount the women were to receive from the Victim's Life Insurance.
AAA
When running over the victim McDavid, the fuel line became disconnected
They had to call Auto Club for a tow.
The membership on the card was paid by Golay.
The undercarriage of the car was examined.
Traces of blood were found matching McDavid's DNA.
Both were convicted of Murder Both sentenced to LIFE without Parole

CHAPTER 26 WHAT HAVE WE LEARNED?

Many people who hear this story about these two elderly women shake their heads in disbelief. We tend to think of women as being the type who nurture others and are non-threatening. Especially the grandmotherly types, who want to be helpful and comfort those around them. When one listens to the two women talking in the police interview room, there is no sympathy or empathy in their voices. The only time Helen talked about the victims was when she was trying to convince Olga to say that Kenneth McDavid loved them and wanted them to have the benefit of all the life insurance policies. Helen went on to remind Olga that their preconceived story was that McDavid was so pleased that the women made him feel a part of their family.

One could say that Helen had no conscience, but it is more than that. Helen had a value system in which 'Homeless Men' had no worth. Her feeling was that they didn't contribute to society so they had no value. Killing a homeless person wasn't like killing a human being. It was like hoeing weeds. When you get rid of the weeds the garden grows and flourishes.

Several books have been written and TV movies made about the two elderly women. In February 2010, one book came out titled the ***Black Widow Murders***. Several TV programs have been produced, such as ***Deadly Women – Behind the Mask*** in September 2009 and in November 2013, **Elder Skelter- Death, Lies, and Security Tape**.

Both women appealed their conviction. The main issue contested was the fact that the prosecution used a supervisor from the Coroner's Office to testify to the conclusion of the toxicology report. He wasn't the person who actually conducted the test. The defendants claimed that they were denied their right to confront and cross-examine since the person who conducted the test didn't testify.

This was a highly debated constitutional issue. Eventually the California Supreme Court considered the case and found that the actions of the prosecution were proper and that even if it wasn't, there was sufficient other evidence to affirm the convictions of both Helen Golay and Olga Rutterschmidt.

CHAPTER 27 EPILOGUE

Helen Golay

Now housed at Central California Women's Facility in Chowchilla, CA.

Olga Rutterschmidt

Now housed at Central California Women's Facility in Chowchilla, CA.

Jimmy Collins

He is fortunate to be alive. His good judgment saved him when the women started treating him like an object and not a person. He saw the handwriting on the wall that he was being used. As a once-homeless man, he has turned his life around and sees daylight at the end of the tunnel.

Truc Do

She is a remarkable individual who was a political refugee from Vietnam and came to the U.S. with her family before the fall of Saigon in 1975. Her family placed high emphasis on education, and Truc Do went to UCLA, graduating Magna Cum Laude with College Honors. She went to Stanford Law School, where she graduated in 1997. After passing the California State Bar exam, she joined the Los Angeles DA's Office, where she was recognized as an exceptional trial attorney.

She assisted in the prosecution of the Michael Demirdjian case, which involved the stoning to death of two young teenagers over a drug deal that had gone bad. Her 12-year career as a prosecutor saw her trying a number of high-publicity cases. In 2010 she left the DA's Office, after she was able to convict Phil Spector for the murder of Lana Clarkson. Then she went into private practice and became a trial lawyer and partner in the Los Angeles office of Munger, Tolles and Olson.

Bobby Grace

He is a seasoned trial attorney continuing to work as a prosecutor for the DA's Office. He is highly respected by his colleagues, adversaries, and especially the judges. His low-key mannerisms make him especially persuasive with jurors. He has a reputation that he can handle any type of murder case, even the last minute handoffs. With all the years of experience he has seen, nothing overwhelms him. He possesses an uncanny confidence that makes him a great litigator. He has a sterling reputation for fairness and has been given the new position of reviewing old convictions for Innocent Defendants. The DA's Office has been fortunate that he has remained a prosecutor, since he has had numerous opportunities to be appointed a judge and certainly could make twice as much money in a private law firm.

Det. Dennis Kilcoyne

He finally retired from LAPD Robbery Homicide Division, although he continued for a while to assist in the famous Grim Sleeper Murder case. He was the guiding force behind many of the notorious homicide cases that were solved by hard-noise detective work. His sixth sense of solving cases will be sorely missed by the RHD and especially the DA's Office.

Graphic of Sante Kimes, the next Old Lady Killer we will discuss.

Graphics11

KIMES CASE

Infamous mother son duo

Sante Kimes **Kenny Kimes**
(Loving Mother) **(Devoted Son)**

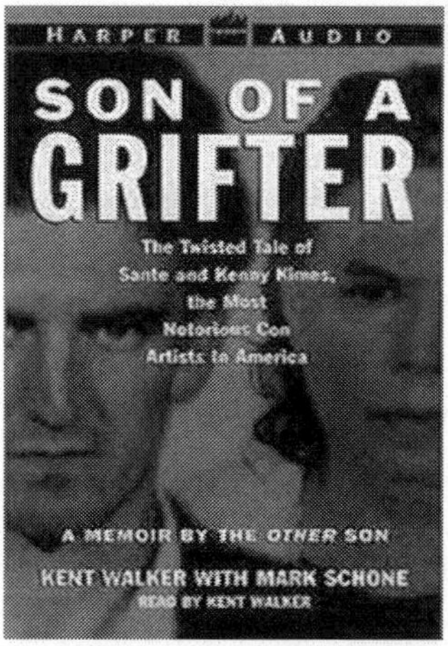

Books, TV and Movies have been made about their lives.

CHAPTER 28 ANOTHER WICKED WOMAN

You, the reader, have now been introduced to Helen and Olga, who were killers in their 70s. The question becomes, how likely is it to find other women in their 60s and 70s who are killers? What is ironic is how the LA District Attorney's Office had another similar case shortly before the Helen and Olga case. That case was the notorious **Sante Kimes** case. Sante was 65 when she and her 25-year-old son, Kenny Jr., were killing people all across the country. Sante never received the mother-of-the-year award, since she was a ruthless mother who terrorized her children and even had an erratic or **erotic relationship** with her son, Kenny. She gained the reputation of being one of the most devious and diabolical con artists of recent times. She had a compulsive personality to manipulate and to control others around her.

The Sante Kimes case took place in 1998, around the time Helen and Olga were taking out insurance policies on their first victim, Paul Vados. Unfortunately, **1998** was a gloomy year for all of us in that old 'Blue Eyes,' Frank Sinatra, died at 82. Most of us grew up with his music and thought he and his songs would live forever. Just like many of us who loved Western movies were saddened when Roy Rogers passed away at 86. Most young boys idolized and wanted to be like Roy or possibly Gene Autry. One of the common trivia questions of all times is to name Roy's horse, which most people remember as Trigger. (Interesting that Trigger is stuffed and resides in a museum. Few remember the name of Gene Autry's horse. Hint: He was a Champion).

Also, in 1998 many famous entertainers passed away. Sonny Bono died in a ski accident, which showed us the dangers of skiing through the trees in the forests. As exhilarating as it is to swish between the tall trees in the snow-covered forest, most of us have stopped that thrill by returning to the main ski slopes. Every time Cher has a 'Goodbye Tour,' one can't help remembering Sonny and Cher holding little Chasity's hand while singing "I've Got You Babe." Well, 1998 was a sad year for many of us, but let's review how an older woman by the name of Sante Kimes made it an even sadder year for her murder victims' families. We will review two of the murder cases involving Sante.

(Many if not most of you readers have read books or seen TV programs about Sante Kimes. I don't want to retell her lengthy story, but I want to provide you with a short review of Sante's life. This will give us an opportunity to compare Sante Kimes to Helen Golay and Olga Rutterschmidt. There are numerous uncanny similarities between these three dames.)

Sante was a self-proclaimed criminal who thrived on committing crime despite the lack of motive or need for the theft. She had a habit of stealing to satisfy an inexplicable need that never seemed to be fulfilled. She was proud of her proficiency to lie to others about the crimes. She was like an addict who couldn't get enough of a thrill in trying to outsmart, outwit, and outfox anyone she came in contact with. It seemed a logical conclusion that her scams and thievery would progress to murder.

It is weird how a loving mother and an obedient son became known as the 'Gruesome Twosome' as they crisscrossed the country leaving peaceful towns in shambles from their fraudulent scams.

She was born in July 1934 and was named Sante Louise Singhrs. Her roots were planted in Oklahoma City in the heart of the Dust-Bowl with a family consisting of an East Indian father and a Dutch mother. Rounding out the family were four siblings. They all migrated to Los Angeles, where their father deserted the family. In order to survive, her mother brought in money for the family by working as a prostitute. Eventually, the family dissolved as a unit and the children rotated from orphanages to foster homes. Sante's family life was truly dysfunctional; however, by the time Sante was 12 years old she had the good fortune of being adopted by a stable family that moved to Carson City, Nevada. During her latter teenage years she did well in school and was involved in all the normal school activities. Life seemed to be good for Sante, and during those years she was known as Sandy Chambers.

The high school she attended and the experiences she had possibly were the turning point in her life. She was attractive and the boys were crazy about her and she enjoyed all the attention. However, prior to graduation Sante was caught shoplifting at a local five-and-dime store. (For those who don't remember, such businesses were a form of a variety store selling a wide range of inexpensive household goods. They went by names like Woolworth's, Kress, Newberry's, and Ben Franklin). Sante received a break in that she was not prosecuted for her transgression. Shoplifting may have been a disastrous mistake in her life. It appears that the lesson she learned from the shoplifting experience was it was OK to steal as long as you are good at talking your way out of it. Unfortunately, she wasn't deterred from stealing and learned how to glide under the radar. She felt there were no consequences, so she continued to steal by using her adopted father's credit card.

Her high school graduation was a pivotal point in that she had the prospect of going to college to study journalism. However, she took a different road that included marrying a school sweetheart. As romantic as such a match should be, the marriage lasted all of three months. She didn't seem to learn anything from that bad experience in that as soon as the divorce was final, she immediately married another high school admirer. That marriage lasted a little longer as well as produced a child by the name of Kent. Her husband stuck it out for several years, but he gave up on Sante as she continued to steal from others and commit shoplifting. There is an English word that describes Sante's behavior and that is **kleptomaniac**.

After the second divorce, she recognized that she had made some bad choices and returned to Los Angeles, where her main occupation was prostitution and stealing. Her proficiency as a larcenist was remarkable. Some might say that Sante was a **thief with BALLS**. To give you an example, one day Sante went into a Cadillac dealership and asked the salesman if she could take a **'test drive'** in one of their new Cadillacs. She talked the salesman into letting her take the car on her own. She projected the appearance of a business woman who wanted to really test the car without being bothered with a lot of sales talk. The salesman didn't see any harm in giving this young damsel the keys for a drive around the block. Needless to say, Sante continued to drive the car for months before she was caught. When the police officer asked her what she was doing with the Cadillac, she nonchalantly said, "I was merely **'test driving'** the car as I told the salesman I wanted to do."

She didn't want to give up the incredible high she felt every time she pulled off a successful theft. To her it was an adrenaline rush that she was addicted to. As time went by, Sante was looking for a more stable life. One day, out of nowhere, came a 'knight on the white horse' and his name was **Kenneth Kimes Sr**. He was the perfect person for Sante in a peculiar way. He was from Oklahoma and migrated to California, where he started working the fields as a melon picker in the Central valleys. His life was like Horatio Alger's: a person who worked hard, saved his money, and became enormously prosperous.

He went into the construction business and carved a niche for himself by building motels in the 1950s. He had calculated that people were starting to travel by using their cars and they no longer wanted to stay in hotels but wanted to enjoy the comforts of the motels. He built over 30 motels and even built the Mecca Motel across from the entrance to Disneyland. The bottom line was that he had made millions of dollars. He was married with a wife and two children, a son and daughter, but he relished womanizing.

Eventually his wife had enough and the marriage ended in a divorce. He was a person who always wanted to be in control. Sante came along and knew exactly how to deal with Mr. Kimes. She would make sure his beverage glass was always full. When he became drunk, Sante took over and was completely in control of him. Even though he was 18 years older than Sante, she wasn't intimidated in the least. The two of them were ideal for each other. He came to the table with millions in cash and real estate. She brought to the relationship cunningness that allowed them to go from one scam to another, always making money.

In 1975, when Sante was 40 years old, she and Kenneth Senior had a son who was named Kenneth Junior (Kenny). They, as a couple, didn't get married until Kenny was six years old. They maintained homes in Honolulu, La Jolla, Palm Springs, Santa Barbara, and a special house in Las Vegas.

CHAPTER 29 THE TEAM OF KENNETH SR. AND SANTE

Kenneth Sr. and Sante lived well together and didn't need to steal. The couple loved the thrill of committing frauds, thefts, filing lawsuits, and suing people. Fires 'mysteriously' occurred at their homes, followed by efforts to collect on the fire insurance policies. An illustration of the boldness of the two was when they fraudulently gained access into the White House during a reception given by President Gerald Ford. Outsmarting the Secret Service was an extraordinary achievement for them. They were so proud of the White House photograph of them shaking hands with the President that it truly became a collector's item.

Sante had a love affair with Cadillacs, diamonds, and fur coats. She liked to impersonate Elizabeth Taylor and enjoyed being mistaken for that celebrity. One day in February 1980, Sante and Kenneth were staying at the Mayflower Hotel in Washington D.C. That evening they went down to the Mayflower Town and Country lounge. Mrs. Kenworth was there and had taken off her dark ranch mink coat and placed it over a chair next to where she was seated. Kenneth Sr. went over to distract Mrs. Kenworth as Sante slithered behind to slip on the fur coat. Sante returned to where she had been sitting and put on her own fur coat over Mrs. Kenworth's $6,500 fur coat.

People at another table saw what happened and were stunned at what they were observing in front of them. When Mrs. Kenworth discovered her coat was missing, the police were called. The witnesses to the incident gave a description of the suspect as the lady that looked like Elizabeth Taylor. The hotel staff were only too familiar with that lady and told the police the woman was staying in a room up on the 7th floor. Then the police went to the Kimes' hotel room, where they knocked and the door was answered by Mr. Kimes. The police could see a fur coat on the bed so they entered. Inside, they found Mrs. Kenworth's mink coat lying on the bed with her name tag cut out with a razor blade. While looking around the room, the police found several additional mink coats as well as a man's tall overcoat with the owners' names cut off.

Sante was arrested and prosecuted for the theft of the fur coat. She used excuse after excuse to have the case continued time after time. It took five years before the case actually went to trial for stealing the fur coat. When the jury reached a verdict, Sante was nowhere to be found. So the judge took the verdict, which was guilty as charged, without Sante being present. Later Sante appeared and claimed she was in an accident and had gone home for medical attention. She appealed her conviction on the basis that she was convicted in absentia and that was illegal. Later the appellate court agreed with Sante and the conviction was thrown out.

She was like the 'Teflon Woman' to which nothing stuck. However, her next caper changed her life forever. Sante and Kenneth were constantly traveling to Mexico, and they would bring back numerous young girls as maids. They would use them around the house as servants and kept them locked up so they couldn't leave.

While Sante was consumed with her lengthy trial over the fur coat, several of the girls escaped the house and went to authorities. As a result, Kenneth and Sante were prosecuted on human slavery charges. Prior to trial, Kenneth Sr. accepted a deal and pled guilty and was sentenced to attend an alcohol treatment program.

Sante went to trial in Las Vegas and seven of the Mexican girls testified to the atrocities that she had committed on the girls. The maids stated they were never paid, never permitted to take days off, nor were they allowed to contact relatives. They told the court they received physical and other types of abuse mainly from Sante Kimes. Sante was convicted and sentenced to five years in federal prison. That sentence changed Sante forever.

While Sante was in prison, her 15-year-old son, Kenny, blossomed. He and his father began spending time together, establishing a bond that was never there when Sante was on the scene. For Kenny's birthday his father built a large swimming pool in the back yard of their house in Las Vegas. For the first time Kenny was able to associate with the neighboring young people. He was permitted to go to public schools. For years the family traveled so much that Kenny had to be home schooled with various tutors. This period of time, while his mother was in prison, gave him a chance to be a normal kid and have friends. While Sante was away, Kenny had no contact with his mother and expressed hatred for her and felt ashamed for what she had done.

In 1989, after serving three years in prison, she was released. The prison authority hoped the prison experience was harsh enough on Sante to deter her from committing crimes in the future. However, for Sante it was a definite learning experience for an entirely different reason. She hated being in prison and vowed never to return. From that point on, Sante would do anything to make sure she didn't go back to prison. To Sante it didn't mean walking the straight and narrow but that there would be no witnesses to testify against her. In other words, from that point on in Sante's life, **all witnesses who could testify against her had to be killed**.

As soon as Sante was out of prison in 1989, she and Kenneth Sr. were up to their old scams of burning down their property to collect on the fire insurance. They torched their Honolulu house, but the fire insurance company resisted paying the accidental fire claim. Sante demonstrated her new philosophy when the feds were getting close to making an arson case against her and Kenneth. The feds had persuaded the Kimes' attorney to become an informant for the feds. When Sante started feeling the heat of possible arson charges against her, she and Kenneth Sr. invited their attorney friend (the new informant for the feds) to join them on a delightful vacation to Costa Rica. He joined them on the flight down. However, strangely he never returned and as a matter of fact, he was never seen alive again. Now since the arson investigation lacked the key witness, the investigation was soon terminated as Sante and Kenneth Sr. walked away free as two love birds.

Unfortunately, Sante's release from prison was devastating for Kenny Jr.. He had grown and matured during the three years his mother was away in prison. He had enjoyed his father's less controlling ways and living in a stable household. Kenny wanted to get away from his mother, so he worked hard to be admitted to the University of Santa Barbara where he could be independent of his mother. It didn't last long, since Mommy decided to move to Santa Barbara with her husband. Sante wanted to be involved in every phase of Kenny's life. The residential area for the University was called Isla Vista, and on weekends it turned into a 'Party Town.' When Kenny had a party at his apartment, Sante would supply the beer kegs. She would attend his parties and often ended up as the life of the party. During this period, Kenny's hatred for his mother softened and the relationship evolved into more of incestuous liaison.

By this time Sante seemed to be showing more interest in her son's exciting life than her boring life with her 77-year-old husband. Then in 1994, Sante drove to the bank in downtown Santa Barbara with her husband, Kenneth Sr. He remained in the car as she went into the bank to make a deposit, and when she came out her husband was dead in the parked car. It was claimed to be a heart attack, and whether it was or not no one knew for sure. At the time of Kenneth Sr.'s death, Kenny Jr. was on spring break in Hawaii. Sante flew to Hawaii to join her son and together they spread her husband's ashes on the placid waves of the Pacific.

Kenny Jr. was the only member of the family who knew that Kenneth Sr. had died. The reason for the secrecy was that Sante was never able to convince Kenneth Sr. to write a new Will removing his older children from the existing Will. Whenever his older children asked about their father, Kenneth Sr., Sante would say he was on a business trip in Japan. In the meantime, Sante went on a campaign to transfer over much of the property into her name or into names she had control over.

Sante moved back to Las Vegas to permanently live in the house on Geronimo Way. The Vegas place was a comfortable two-story house at the end of the development which overlooked the golf course. From the master bedroom they had a gorgeous view of manicured lawns covering the rolling hills with various pine trees that provided shade on the fairways. The back yard had a curved swimming pool with a delightful spa. Sante loved to soak in the spa while watching the country club crowd sauntering down the fairways behind their backyard.

Las Vegas was the perfect city for Sante to call home. Her house was a short drive from the Vegas strip, where the saying goes that 'what happens in Vegas stays in

Vegas.' She fit in with the scammers and hustlers, which Vegas was full of. Sante understood human nature just like the casinos on the strip. Everyone understands that all the games are rigged so the house ultimately wins. The marketing concept is that certain lucky people can beat the house. The idea is to convince all the people that they are those few special people who are WINNERS.

Sante fit in with the Vegas crowd and life was good for her. In order to stay ahead of her creditors and various lawsuits, she had put most of her funds in offshore bank accounts. This was to make sure that others weren't going to get any profit from all the ill-gotten gains that she had made. Unfortunately, the money well eventually went dry when she discovered the bank account in the offshore banks was finally depleted.

The following graphic page shows the various crimes that Sante Kimes was involved in.

Graphics 12

KIMES CASE

Happy Family

Sante & Kenneth Kimes Sr.

The Kimes with son Kenney

Sante stole mink coat in Mayflower Hotel in Washington D.C.

Crashing White House party meeting President Ford

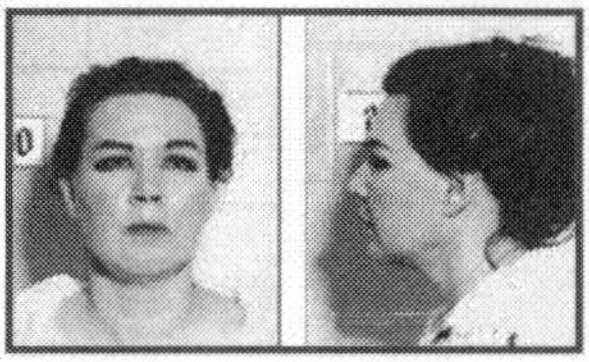

Sante arrested for Slave Trade & mug photos of Sante

CHAPTER 30 SANTE TAKES OVER

Sante didn't want to be a 'Have Not' person. Kenneth Sr. was no longer available to provide the pecuniary support and personal attention that Sante craved. She had no other person to turn to other than her son Kenny. In order to help his mother, Kenny obediently left college and moved to Vegas to be with her. From that point on, Kenny was mama's accomplice. An example how Sante used Kenny was she had him file malpractice lawsuits against a plastic surgeon in San Diego. Kenny filed a complaint stating that the doctor had botched his nose job. He also filed a claim against the doctor on behalf of his mother who claimed that she fell from the operating table during one of her face-lifts and she suffered a traumatic head injury.

Those malpractice lawsuits didn't generate the kind of money Sante needed to live the lifestyle she had grown accustomed to. She and Kenny met with her attorney, Alan Rucker (pseudonym), to find other possible money sources. The attorney suggested one way they could acquire money was by selling some real estate. Years before, the attorney had set up a corporation named 'AGAHAN' to hold title to property in Santa Maria, California, owned by Sante and Kenneth Sr. She was trying to develop the property for a subdivision. A dispute arose and Sante's reaction was to refuse to pay for the plans for the project. A lien was placed on the property, which prevented her from selling the property or receiving any cash out of it.

Since there was no easy way to sell the Santa Maria property, Sante realized her only option was to take out a loan on her residential property on Geronimo Way in Vegas. She had no mortgage on the Vegas property; therefore, it would be easy to obtain a loan. Over the years, to prevent creditors from placing liens on their property, they had transferred title of their residence to a **Mr. David Kazdin**. He had been involved in numerous business ventures with the Kimeses. Kazdin had moved from Las Vegas back to Los Angeles where his daughter lived. Because of all the financial pressure, Sante decided to follow her attorney's advice and take out a home loan on the Geronimo Way house.

Nancy Watson (pseudonym) lived in Las Vegas and worked part-time as a bookkeeper for the Kimeses to assist them with all of their investments. Later, she became a certified Notary in order to facilitate Sante's business transactions. Since the Las Vegas property was truly owned by the Kimeses, she figured that it would be OK for her to have her bookkeeper sign Kazdin's name on the loan application. After affixing Kazdin's signature on all the documentations, the material was sent to the financial company, OCWEN Bank. Thereupon the bank distributed some of the funds from the loan to the bookkeeper's personal bank account. From there, Watson transferred the funds from her account to Sante's offshore bank accounts. In this way, no creditor of Sante could intercept any of that money.

Sante was pleased how easy it was to obtain the loan, so she thought, why not double dip by taking out fire insurance? First, she had to figure out how to obtain the maximum amount of fire insurance on the Las Vegas house. Sante and her late husband, Kenneth Kimes, were professionals at the old scam of burning down their property and collecting on the fire insurance. So the answer was to use someone else's name to obtain the fire insurance. The question was, who could she find who would let her use their name? She went to a homeless shelter and found a transient by the name of Robert McDonald (pseudonym) and persuaded him to come to work for her doing maintenance work on the house and other properties. She agreed to provide food and lodging for him. Part of the agreement was that Sante could use his name in various business transactions. She filled out a Quit Claim Deed showing that David Kazdin had transferred his interest in the residential property to Robert McDonald. Then she used McDonald's name to apply for the fire insurance policy on the house in the maximum amount of $500,000.

The Kimeses' brains worked in devious ways. Sante thought what a waste to burn up all their luxurious furniture. Even though they were going to claim the furniture as a loss for insurance purposes, they thought why not move out the good furniture before the fire. Kenny's task was to find a storage unit and have the furniture relocated there. Kenny couldn't do all the heavy lifting by himself so he hired a gentleman by the name of Stanley Peters to help him. Days before the fire, they went to the Vegas house and cherry-picked the best pieces of furniture and took them to a rental storage unit.

In order to establish an alibi, Kenny and Sante took their maintenance man, Robert McDonald, to Los Angeles, where they stayed in a motel. On one of the evenings, Kenny quietly slipped away to return to Vegas to torch the house. After the fire was set, Kenny quickly returned to LA before McDonald knew he was even gone. The next day, the Kimeses were notified that their Vegas house had burned under suspicious circumstances. Shortly thereafter, the Kimeses had their maintenance man, Robert McDonald, file a claim for the fire damage of $500,000, which included the fire damage to the structure and the contents.

Taking out the loan had paid off for Sante, and it was just a matter of time before they would have the fire insurance money. Sante had done everything right and was proud of her meticulous planning of all contingencies. She had been very careful in her dealings with the OCWEN Bank. She made sure that all correspondence about the loan would be sent to her residence on Geronimo Way, Las Vegas.

However, Murphy's Law seemed to haunt Sante. Somehow one of the employees at OCWEN Bank went through all the loan paperwork and missed the small piece of paper instructing that all correspondence be sent to the Las Vegas address instead of Kazdin's house in Granada Hills, CA. The employee automatically sent the mortgage monthly payment book to David Kazdin's house.

The result was that when David Kazdin received the loan payment book he immediately was on the phone to the bank, asking them what loan they were talking about. He followed that up by sending the bank a letter explaining that he hadn't taken out any such loan and he hadn't signed off on any property in Las Vegas. Needless to say, this made the bank quite nervous and it froze the distribution of the funds for the loan. Instantaneously, the bank started an investigation into the matter. Sante became aware of the mix-up when the bookkeeper, Watson, indicated that the mortgage bank had frozen her personal bank account where she had transferred some of the money from the loan. Sante grasped the situation that she had 'opened a can of worms' and the fastest and best way to rectify it was to have Kazdin sign a quitclaim deed to McDonald, then the bank would leave him alone.

To carry out this new strategy, Sante and Kenny left Vegas with Nancy Watson and they traveled to Kazdin's house in Granada Hills, CA. They parked out of sight of

Kazdin's house and had Watson approach his front door. She rang the doorbell and Kazdin's daughter answered the door and let her in. Watson started discussing with David Kazdin about signing a quit-claim deed on the Vegas property. He denied any knowledge of a loan. She indicated her bank account had been frozen because of the problem of title to the Las Vegas property.

The conversation didn't go well and in short order Nancy Watson left Kazdin's house without obtaining his signature. When she returned to Sante and Kenny in the Town Car, she told them about his refusal. Sante became furious. Then it was time to go to Plan B, which was to find a way to eliminate Kazdin. In order to carry that out, they decided to return to Las Vegas. There, Kenny contacted Stanley Peters about the possibility of obtaining a handgun. Stanley had numerous guns and he showed them to Kenny and explained the benefits of each one. After a lengthy discussion, Kenny selected a .22 caliber handgun and paid Stanley for it.

While in Las Vegas, Kenny went to the homeless shelter to find someone whom he could use to help in the killing. There were several transients at the shelter. Kenny wanted someone who would be reliable and someone who he could count on in doing a killing. Some of the homeless seemed too old and feeble. Others seemed to be wasted on alcohol. Kenny needed someone he could trust but at the same time, someone who would be willing to commit a murder. The task of finding the right person wasn't easy. Then he spotted Sonny Lane (pseudonym), who was younger and had a shady look. Kenny struck up a conversation with him. There seemed to be some type of chemistry between them. Kenny didn't tell Sonny what he would be expected to do, but Kenny was comfortable with his selection.

CHAPTER 31 GOOD DAY FOR A MURDER

On Friday, March 13, 1998, Sante knew that Kazdin was having an Open House in the afternoon trying to sell his Granada Hills home. Kazdin was hoping that Friday the 13th would be his lucky day for selling his place so he could move to Florida. Could Friday the 13th be so unlucky that he would end up dead?

Kenny and Sonny Lane (the new homeless man) drove to Kazdin's place. They both knocked on the door and Kazdin opened it. As Sonny stepped in Kenny came in from behind. Immediately Kenny started talking about the loan situation. Kazdin didn't want to have anything to do with the loan or the Las Vegas property.

Kazdin, for whatever reason, walked back into the kitchen, and Kenny followed directly behind him. Covertly, Kenny stuck his hand into his pocket and slowly pulled out a handgun. Kazdin's attention was looking toward the kitchen he was entering. Kenny placed the gun to the rear of Kazdin's head and pulled the trigger. That was all that was needed to kill Kazdin. A small-caliber bullet from a .22 can be even more deadly than a larger-caliber bullet. What happens with the .22 bullet is it penetrates the skull and continues to bounce off the walls of the interior of the skull and crisscrosses the cerebral cortex to cause extensive injury to the brain. Since the

.22 caliber bullet doesn't have enough velocity to exit the skull, there isn't any collateral damage to the surroundings such as the kitchen.

Sonny Lane was shocked at the shooting, since Kenny hadn't explained all the details about the job. In order to dispose of the body, Kenny instructed Sonny to drive Kazdin's Jaguar into the garage so they could place his body in the trunk of his car. Sonny wasn't familiar with driving a Jaguar so he ran into a planter next to the driveway, causing damage to the rear bumper of the car. Eventually, Sonny pulled the Jaguar into the garage and Kenny closed the garage door. The garage was connected to the house by a hallway, and the two carried Kazdin's body from the kitchen into the garage.

This was a piece of cake until they got into the garage. The challenge was how to get the body into the trunk. The Jaguar extended the full length of the garage. With the garage door down, the only way to get on the other side of the car was to climb over the hood of the car. Kenny looked hurriedly at his watch and could see that the Open House 'lookie loos' would soon be arriving. Kenny instantaneously jumped on top of the hood of the car and told Sonny to lift Kazdin's body up to him. Kenny, by standing on top of the hood, dragged the body across the hood and dropped it on the other side. Kenny climbed down and yelled at Sonny to follow him.

What was sad about all these scratching and dents was that this Jaguar had been Kazdin's pride and joy. When he drove it, he would never park it near other cars in a shopping center parking lot. He was always willing to walk the additional distance just to make sure no one scratched his classic Jaguar. Now the car had two big dents from Kenny's shoe prints on the hood. In addition, it had a dent in the rear fender from when they tried to pull the car into the garage.

Kenny quickly reached inside the car to push the button to pop the trunk open. Then they hastily picked up Kazdin's body and dropped it into the trunk. They returned to the house to clean up any blood on the floor. Because of using a small caliber gun, there was very little blood, and Kenny tried to wipe up any blood he could see on the floor. Since the handgun was an automatic, Kenny had to lean down on his hands and knees to find the single shell casing. It had rolled under the kitchen cabinets, where he picked it up and placed it into his pocket.

Kenny was convinced that they had cleaned the crime scene, so both walked outside and went to the large garage door and opened it. Sonny was instructed to drive the Jaguar with the body in it and Kenny would drive the car they had come in. Sonny very carefully backed the Jaguar out of the garage into the street. He slipped the car into drive and started to follow Kenny in his Lincoln Town Car. Sonny, the homeless man who had been living in a shelter until several days before, was slightly traumatized driving an expensive Jaguar vehicle. But he was especially nervous because he had a dead body in the trunk. He was petrified that he might be stopped by a police officer. When he came to a stop sign he obediently stopped all the way back at the 'Limit Line' before he would enter the intersection.

They proceeded over to the 405 Freeway and then headed southbound toward Los Angeles Airport (LAX). It was still mid-morning, and rush hour traffic had thinned out except for the interchange with the Interstate 10 near Westwood. They drove to the airport, exited, and continued to the Westchester shopping center. There they pulled into the parking lot and parked near the rear. Kenny got out and walked over to Sonny and told him to park and lock up the Jaguar, since they had to wait until it was dark in order to get rid of the body.

That meant that Kenny and Sonny had to find a way to pass eight hours before it would be dark. What should two killers do to kill time? They both got in the Lincoln and drove to the Beverly Center Shopping Center, about 10 miles away. There they spent a leisurely day having a pleasant lunch. Afterward, they wandered through the shopping center, mainly window shopping. Since they still had to wait, they went to the cinema complex to watch several recent movies. Some of the hits playing were *Saving Private Ryan*, which Kenny didn't care to see; and *There's Something about Mary*, which he didn't want to see since he heard it was a 'Girl Flick.' The only movie that appealed to Kenny was *The Man With The Iron Mask*, so they purchased two tickets and a large bag of popcorn and found seats near the back. For the next two hours they escaped into a make-believe world while waiting to dispose of a body.

As the City of the Angels darkened for evening, they headed back to the airport area. Kenny drove the Lincoln Town Car to Westchester and at the parking lot pulled up next to the Jaguar that had footprint dents on the hood. Kenny told Sonny to follow him to a neglected apartment complex that he was familiar with. Kenny headed east, then slightly south, which was directly under the flight path of LAX North Runway. Kenny slowly drove down the rear alley, which had numerous trash dumpsters pushed into the alley for trash pick-up for the next day. Kenny was driving slowly as he looked around to see if anyone from the apartments could see them in the alley. The headlights of the Lincoln Town Car had spotted a dumpster that was well shielded by a set of detached apartments. Kenny motioned to Sonny to pull up to the dumpster so the trunk of the Jaguar would be next to it.

Kenny parked the Lincoln on the other side of the alley next to a closed business area. Kenny continued to wave to Sonny to back the Jaguar even closer to the dumpster. Sonny cautiously got out of the Jaguar and waited for Kenny to gesture to him to pop the trunk open. Kenny made sure that both of the lids of the dumpster were open. Kenny nodded to Sonny and he leaned into the car and pushed the trunk button. Suddenly the trunk lid was open revealing a body partially covered in garbage bags. Kenny quickly leaned in and pulled the two trash bags together so the body wouldn't be noticeable.

Kenny tried lifting the body and realized this was a two man job. He told Sonny to come over to help. Sonny hesitated for a moment. He hadn't signed up for killing or dumping bodies. Kenny firmly stated to Sonny, "Come on, let's get this over with." Sonny knew that Kenny still had the gun and he didn't want to end up like this corpus in the trunk. He leaned into the trunk and helped to pick up the body. They had to raise it high enough to reach over the side of the dumpster. While they were attempting to do this, the garbage bags continue to slide off the body. This was disappointing for Kenny. While resting the body on the top of the dumpster, Kenny tried to pull one of the garbage bags to cover up the victim's head. He did his best and told Sonny on the count of three to toss the body all the way into the trash-filled dumpster.

As they let go, they heard Kazdin's body crash into the dumpster, crushing some cardboard boxes, and the clink of some bottles and cans falling to the bottom of the dumpster. Earlier, Kenny had taken out all of Kazdin's identification from his wallet and told Sonny that he would dispose of them elsewhere. Kenny wasn't thrilled with his immediate task, which included reaching into the dumpster and picking up trash to be placed over the body. He walked away from the dumpster and wiped his hands together as though he was cleaning them.

He directed Sonny to follow him. He got back into the Town Car and drove slowly down to the end of the alley where he saw another dumpster. The Lincoln came to a halt and he opened the door and went over and lifted up the lid of the dumpster with his right hand. With his left hand he tossed Kazdin's wallet and all his identification into the dumpster. He glanced in to make sure that it had fallen in. He could see that it had landed on top of a bag of dirty baby diapers in a Pampers box. Even in the dark of night, the dumpster reeked of noxious odors.

Kenny quickly dropped the lid and it clanged shut. Kenny thought to himself "Why did I have to make so much noise?" As Kenny slowly walked back to the Lincoln he could see the headlights of the Jaguar shining directly on him. At that moment a huge 747 jet came roaring overhead so loud he seemed to freeze in his tracks from the intense sound. Kenny stepped into the Town Car and sat down and closed the door. He looked up at the rearview mirror and could see the pitch black of the alley with the dumpster with the dead body in it. He smiled to himself and wondered if that was the way the mob did it during the Godfather days.

Then Kenny motioned to Sonny to follow him back to the airport shopping center parking lot. There they pulled into a remote section and Sonny locked up the Jaguar and got in the Lincoln. Kenny gave one last look at the Jag and gunned the Town Car engine as though he was glad to get out of there. He drove back to the 405 Freeway heading to the Sherman Oaks/Encino area. For the next five miles Kenny drove up the 405 Freeway with little interference from other traffic. As they got to the Ventura Boulevard off ramp, they maneuvered into the left lane and then headed west. At the corner of Ventura Boulevard and Haskell Avenue, Kenny pulled over and stopped at the rear parking lot of a florist. Kenny scrambled out of the car and said to Sonny, "I'll be back in a few minutes."

The following graphic page show the killing of David Kazdin & disposing of his body.

Graphics 13

KAZDIN KILLING
(March 14, 1998)

David Kazdin Victim   Kazdin's house in Granada Hills   Sante Kimes   Kenny Kimes

Kenny shot the victim in his kitchen & used victim's car to transport body to LAX

Kenny dumped the victim's body in a dumpster near LAX

This was Sante's Vegas residence that she had burned down for the insurance money

CHAPTER 32 MOTHER-SON TEAM

Sheepishly Kenny entered the back door of the small florist shop. The lady came to the counter and asked, "How can I help you?" Kenny looked around to see if he could point out a special flower arrangement. Nothing caught his attention, so he tried to explain what he was looking for. He told her, "I would like some flowers to celebrate a big event." She said, "Is it something for a birthday or anniversary? He said, "No, something like a graduation or doing something well." She said, "You mean a Celebration Bouquet." He didn't want to tell her the truth, that it was to commemorate a successful killing of an old associate of the family. He just told her a 'Celebration Bouquet' would do.

In 15 minutes she amazingly created an arrangement that met all of Kenny's expectations. Kenny gave a broad smile of approval and paid $100 cash to the clerk. Sonny waited impatiently in the car and wondered what was taking so long, but when Kenny came out with this colorful bouquet, he didn't say a word. Then off they went, taking Sepulveda up to Mulholland Drive then over to the Bel Air house where the Kimeses were renting rooms. As Kenny walked in, Sante had the TV on and slowly stood up and asked, "How did it go?"

Kenny strolled over to his dear mother and handed her the 'Celebration Bouquet.' He said, "Everything is Okay." A huge smile lit up Sante's face as she said, "What a wonderful son!" Mother-son love never shined so bright as it did at that moment between Sante and Kenny. For the rest of the evening everyone decompressed from all the excitement of a day in which a murder had been successfully committed.

Kenny was well aware of the family slogan—'No Body, No Crime.' Kenny knew that trash dumpsters are never checked by the trash-truck operator. So when you dump a body in a dumpster it is picked up by a trash truck, which takes it to a landfill where it is dumped, and at the end of the day three feet of topsoil is covered on top of the trash. In other words, the body is well buried so it will never ever be found.

However, apparently Kenny wasn't aware of the new sport of **'Dumpster Diving.'** It might not be a legitimate sport, but many people do it with the belief that 'One man's trash can be another man's treasure.' The morning after the disposing of the body in the dumpster, a homeless man was looking in the dumpsters before the big trash trucks arrived to pick up the rubbish. He jumped into the dumpster and he saw these trash bags covering something. The homeless man figured that there must be something valuable inside. He pulled off the top garbage bag and discovered the head of a dead man. He was hoping for some beer or soda cans, not a dead body. He jumped out of the dumpster with lightning speed and scurried to a nearby apartment complex to find someone who would permit him to use their phone to call the police.

The police arrived and checked out the dumpster and sure enough, the homeless man was right. They found a dead body in the dumpster. A cursory search of the pockets didn't reveal any identification. The detectives were brought in to figure out who could this victim be and why was he killed. Because of the age of the victim, it didn't seem to be a gang-related killing. It could be a robbery, but robbers don't dispose of bodies in dumpsters. The one shot in the back of the head by a small-caliber gun didn't add up. There weren't any security cameras in the area to help piece together the identity of the suspect. The way the body was covered indicated the killer didn't intend for the victim to be found. The Dumpster Diver's unexpected discovery had given LAPD another 'John Doe' homicide. It seemed this murder was going to join all the other Cold Cases that accumulate over a year.

What are the chances that another Dumpster Diver would be working in the same area on the same day? Maybe it was the poor economy or the notion that apartment people tend to throw away more recyclables. The next day, the police got a call from another 'Dumpster Diver,' who indicated that he had found a wallet full of credit cards and a driver's license for a Mr. David Kazdin. The police were less than excited about checking out a smelly wallet that had been fished out of the bottom of a dumpster filled with dirty diapers, sanitary napkins, and maggot-filled, week-old rotten food.

The responding police officers had to wonder why they were responding to this call of a found wallet. Many people wouldn't have called the police but would merely take anything of value and throw the rest back in the dumpster. For some reason this 'Dumpster Diver' was trying to be a Good Samaritan. Maybe divers should be rewarded with something similar to a Boy Scout merit badge for honesty. But no such recognition was given to either 'Dumpster Diver.'

The officer, with his latex gloves on, thumbed through the wallet and looked at the driver's license and saw a photo of an older man with a full head of white hair. The officer remembered the detectives had mentioned finding the body of an older man just down the alley a block away. The officers contacted the detectives and told them what they had recovered. The detectives were shown the driver's license and, bingo, they then knew who their 'John Doe' was. The detectives then proceeded to converge on David Kazdin's house in Granada Hills.

They looked for blood and didn't find any, at least on their first cursory glance. (A later search revealed a small drop of blood on the kitchen floor next to the wall board.) Kazdin's daughter mentioned that a stranger had come by to talk to her dad several days before. She didn't know what it was all about, but he had mentioned that he had received a mortgage book for a property in Las Vegas. Now the detectives had some clues to work on. What were the chances that two separate 'Dumpster Divers' would make unusual finds that pointed the detectives to a Las Vegas property that had just recently burned down? Without those 'Dumpster Divers,' the victim's body and his wallet would have ended up in a landfill buried forever, under tons of waste, and years later the dump would be transformed into new parkland with unaware children playing over buried bodies.

Kenny and Sante with their homeless associates were still staying in the rented rooms in Bel Air. Kenny's attention was focused on their so-called maintenance worker, Robert McDonald. Kenny was concerned that he might be talking to the other tenants at the house. They had kept him locked up in one of the bedrooms so he couldn't leave or come in contact with others. They had threatened and even beaten him up on occasions to instill fear in him. Then one evening Kenny, Sante, and Sonny Lane took McDonald out for dinner at a restaurant. While everyone was talking at the table, McDonald excused himself to go to the bathroom. The restrooms were situated near the rear door. McDonald saw his opportunity to escape and disappeared into the dark of the night. When Kenny realized what had happened he became paranoid that McDonald would go to the police. The next morning when the landlord appeared unannounced at the house, Kenny freaked out and he immediately decided to leave the Bel Air house they had been renting.

Originally, Kenny was patting himself on the back for a job well done, until the police started coming around asking questions. As proud as Sante was with her son's accomplishments, she knew it was time for them to move on. This mother-son odyssey began a journey that crossed the entire continent of the USA. From that day forward they were described as 'Grifters.'

Earlier in August 1996, Sante and Kenny had flown to the Grand Caymans with Sayed Bilal Ahmed, a Bahraini banker. They set up bank accounts in the Gulf Union Bank in Caymans with a small deposit. The banker was investigating irregularities in that bank. Sante had talked to him about an on-line business venture. On one of the evenings in August, the relatives of Syed Bilal Ahmed said he left their house to discuss business over dinner with the Kimeses. He went over to the Kimeses' hotel room and it was unknown what was discussed, but somehow Bilal knew too much and the Kimeses couldn't afford to have him go to the authorities. After dinner, they slipped a small amount of a so-called 'Date Rape' drug into his drink and within minutes he passed out.

Then Kenny, with the help of Sante, dragged him into the bathroom and placed his head in the bathtub filled to the top with water. Kenny grabbed the banker by the neck and pushed his head down into the lukewarm water. An instinctive reaction forced the head to jerk out of the water. With both hands Kenny forcibly shoved his head back in the water. The victim's head exhaled air bubbles that splashed water onto Kenny's clothing. With a firm grip, Kenny stood over the banker, holding his head beneath the water. Whenever Kenny thought it was long enough, he would let the head up and the victim started making a noise like a cough. Immediately Kenny thrust the head back into the water. For Kenny it seemed like an hour, but after five minutes holding his head under water the banker had no more life left in him.

Afterward, Kenny placed the victim's body in a sleeping bag and late that night carried it out of the hotel. As strange as it may seem, no one was around to notice what he was up to. Kenny carried the body to the edge of the bay where several rowboats were tied up. He dropped the body in the rear of a little rowboat, and after being seated in the boat he removed the oars from each side and placed them in the rowing position. With his entire might, Kenny started rowing away from shore, but because of the weight of the body the boat got stuck on a sand bar. As Kenny was struggling to break free, two police officers were walking by on the beach. They saw Kenny's predicament and offered to push him away. Thanks to their help, he was able to get off the sand bar. Kenny used all his strength pulling on the oars, and he slowly glided away from the beach. Next, he was concerned that the row boat would sink from the weight of the victim's body; therefore, he was careful not to splash any water into the boat.

Eventually he was far enough out where no one could see him. He opened up the sleeping bag and began using rope to tie an anchor to the body. When the anchor was secure, Kenny gently moved the body over the side of the boat. The body started to float until Kenny took the heavy anchor and tossed it as far as he could. As the anchor swiftly disappeared into the water, it sucked the body into the deep blue sea. Just to be on the safe side, Kenny waited for several moments to make sure the body didn't make a reappearance. When he was convinced all was well, he vigorously rowed back to shore. He then went back to the hotel room and told his mother it was time to get out of town.

CHAPTER 33 GRIFTERS ON THE MOVE

Earlier in April of 1998, the Kimeses had bought a green 1997 Lincoln Town Car from a car dealership in Cedar City, Utah and had it delivered to them in Los Angeles. They paid for the car with a check for $14,900. Unfortunately for the salesman, the check bounced as high as a kite. (Later, the dealership had the DA file criminal charges against both Sante and Kenny for fraud and auto theft.)

One of the reasons Kenny had selected the Lincoln Town Car was its amazingly soft, comfortable ride with an incredible high-end sound system. As mom and son glided across the heartland of America, Kenny wanted his mom serenaded by the hits of the day, which were Elton John's ***Candle In The Wind*** and Celine Dion's ***My Heart Will Go On.*** The Lincoln's surround sound was a marvelous feature. Most important for Sante was to be seen traveling in a luxurious car that represented her status in life.

They would put several thousand miles on that Town Car, stretching from Los Angeles to New York by way of Florida. While crossing one of the southern states, they committed another vehicle theft. It wasn't clear why they did this, but when they pulled into a small community they saw a For Sale sign on an enormous, almost-new Recreational Vehicle (RV). Sante and Kenny always had an RV in Las Vegas. However, their RV didn't weather well with all the heat and wind in Vegas. Their RV had passed the point of being reliable. Most people would have traded it in for a newer model. Nevertheless, for Kenny and Sante it was time for another 'con.' They could tell that this backward area hadn't seen a professional scam artist at work for a long time. This RV was listed for $83,000, and Kenny knew how to work the owner. Kenny didn't quibble over the price and agreed with the seller that the RV was worth the asking price. Then Kenny pulled out a checkbook and wrote a check for the full amount so they could take it immediately. The seller received some form of identification and filled out the paperwork for the sale.

Kenny got in the RV and asked all sorts of stupid questions about how to use it. Undoubtedly the seller had to be thinking what a sucker this buyer was. Within an hour, Kenny was driving out of the driveway with an $83,000 RV, and the seller waved good-bye to him. Kenny looked out his side mirror and saw the seller and a slight smirk came over his face. He wondered if the seller would still be smiling when he discovered that the check wasn't worth the paper it was written on. Sante followed in the Lincoln behind Kenny as he made his way to the interstate heading for Florida and disappearing into the sunset.

Several months prior, Sante had attended a seminar in Las Vegas where she met a man who told her about an elderly woman who operated a unique high-end bed and breakfast hotel in New York City. This woman was a wealthy widow who was 82 years old and childless. Sante heard that she also maintained large amounts of cash in her apartment. Sante did a little investigation by using a title company and confirmed that Irene Silverman was the sole owner of the Manhattan property and learned that she owned the property free and clear without any type of mortgage. The fact that she owned this property outright, worth over $8 million, and she had no heirs was a dream come true for a professional conniver, schemer, and plotter like Sante.

Sante couldn't help herself from thinking up some type of scam to get access to that property. First, Sante knew that she needed some type of introduction to meet Irene Silverman. The person indicated that this woman was good friends with Rudy Vaccari, who owned a specialty butcher shop in Manhattan. Sante called the hotel and used the excuse that she was the secretary for Manny Guerra and he wanted to rent an apartment. She was able to contact one of the staff who took down the information, but no formal reservation could be made because Irene was unavailable.

On Saturday, June 13, 1998, Sante and Kenny loaded up the Lincoln Town Car in Florida and started the long drive to New York. They took with them an assistant by the name of Jose Albert (pseudonym), who they employed to do the menial work Sante and Kenny didn't want to do. The three of them headed up Interstate 95. In 1998, this was the main route used by drug dealers to hastily transport narcotics to the Big Apple. The question was whether the large Lincoln Town Car fit the description of possible drug dealers. Kenny and Jose would certainly fit the profile of drug dealers. However, having Sante with her grandmother appearance rounding out the Town Car protected Kenny from being stopped by the police.

As they neared their destination, Kenny pulled off Interstate 95 and drove through the streets of New Jersey. As he slowly cruised through an industrial area. he pulled the Lincoln over and stopped. Looking over to his right he mumbled to the others, "That's a perfect place to dump a body." Jose Albert looked in the direction of this grassy field and wondered what he was referring to. Although Albert traveled with them to New York, he was not privy to what was about to happen.

CHAPTER 34 WHO WAS IRENE SILVERMAN?

To understand this new scam that Sante had cooked up, one has to know a little about Irene Silverman. She owned and operated an unusual hotel in the Upper Eastside of New York at 20 East 65th Street near Madison Avenue. This old gray stone mansion had been converted into luxury apartments. The structure was built to give the appearance of a substantial city mansion with its carved stone facade and sturdy wrought iron doors. The building projected opulence contained in a secure environment. Irene rented her rooms to a special clientele with an arty persuasion.

In order to understand the owner of the building, Irene Silverman, one has to go back in time to 1916, when she was born in New Orleans and given the name of Irene Zambelli. Her father was an Italian fishmonger and her dear mother was a Greek seamstress. While growing up she took ballet lessons. When her parents went their separate ways, Irene stayed with her mother and they traveled to New York. Irene studied ballet with the great Michael Fokine and eventually received a job as a dancer in New York. Unfortunately, her ballet career had its limitations. Because of her size of 5' 0" and weighing 98 pounds, she was too short to join a major ballet company. But her shortness didn't prevent her from being a dancer at the Radio City Music

Hall. When the dancers lined up in a long row, Irene was always the last dancer in the row because she was always the shortest.

By being a prominent dancer, she mixed well with the high society of New York. One of the people she was introduced to was an urbane banker named Sam Silverman, who later became one of the most successful mortgage brokers in the country. Shortly thereafter in 1941, they were married, even though he was ten years her senior. As she later explained, the marriage was one of convenience for both. He needed a vivacious wife who had the energy to entertain visitors and clients from his business. She insisted that her mother live with them, which wasn't a concern for him since they had such spacious houses throughout the world.

As a couple they had homes in Paris, Athens, and Honolulu, as well as the gray stone mansion in Manhattan. That palatial building had a ballroom, a replica of Le Petit Trianon Music Room in Versailles with all its marble, oak paneling, and gilding It was furnished with works of art and theatrical memorabilia. The roof contained a lush garden that was enchanting when illuminated at night.

For many years the mansion was her home where she lived with her wealthy husband. However, after he passed away in 1973, the house was much too large for one person. That was when she came up with the idea of dividing up the house into a dozen or so luxury apartments. She described her place as something between a posh hotel and a grand boarding house. She would rent the rooms from $6,000 to $12,000 per month to tycoons and businessmen, show business stars, and interesting artsy types. She wanted her tenants to be fascinating people and she wanted to create an atmosphere of an 18th-century Parisian salon. Irene left the mansion infrequently and only in the company of her staff. The mansion was her pride and joy, and she was financially secure. By 1998, Irene was 83 and was still going strong. Her trademark was dying her hair Lucille Ball orange and entertaining her tenant guests. On some evenings after dinner, she would entertain her guests by rising up on her tiptoes with her hands pointed high above her head and she would do several fouetté turns from Swan Lake.

On the following graphic page are photos of Irene Silverman and her lavish hotel.

Graphics 14

IRENE SILVERMAN

Irene Silver as a ballerina

Brownstone home she inherited

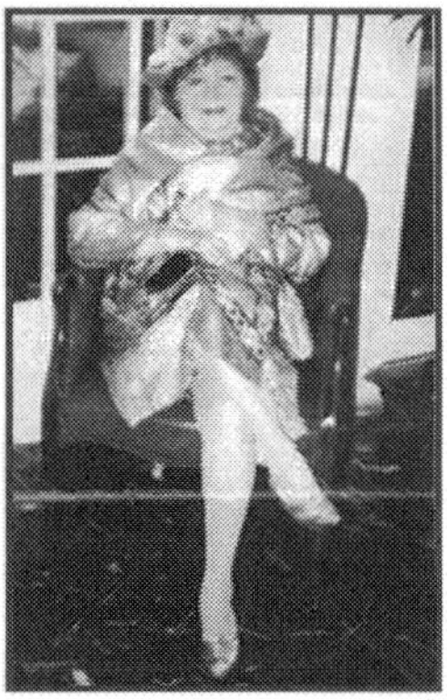

Irene Silverman at 82

Irene created lavish hotel

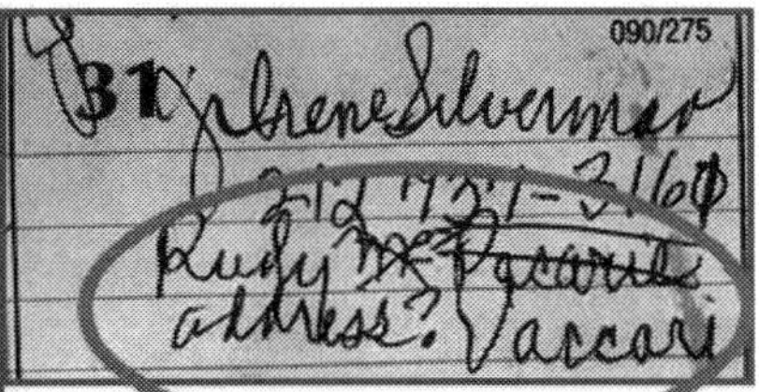

Sante's calendar with name of Irene's butcher

This was Missing Person flier used by police

CHAPTER 35 KENNY GETS FOOT IN THE DOOR

On Sunday, June 14, 1998, a Mr. Manny Guerrin (the alias name Kenny Kimes was using) arrived at Irene Silverman's hotel asking for a room. Well-dressed Kenny turned on his charm and projected the image of a well-spoken member of high society. Irene was impressed, but she had certain standards that she never deviated from. She required her potential tenants to submit a resume with the names and numbers of references. If she didn't know the potential tenants personally, she conducted extensive background checks to verify that the person was of the caliber to fit in with her other avant-garde tenants.

When she requested Manny Guerrin to supply a resume with references, he agreed to provide her with one the next day, since he hadn't brought any paperwork with him on this day. Irene had learned to not make any exceptions. Manny (Kenny) knew that money talked extremely loud with business people. Irene continued to tell him that she had to have his resume before she could rent any room to him. Manny assured her that he understood and dropped the name of her butcher as someone he knew and who had recommended her place to him. As Manny started to leave, he pulled out $6,000 in cash and explained he would be willing to pay her in cash.

Irene Silverman's eyes were captivated by the 60 one-hundred dollar bills. Somehow her mind snapped back to the days she was paid $36.00 per week in cash at the Radio City Music Hall. She indicated that she could make an exception and told him she would get a receipt for him. Within minutes Manny was escorted to apartment 1B on the first floor. Kenny was pleased with his acting ability, and he had accomplished the first part of their plan, which was to get into the mansion and learn how the hotel operated.

Irene's impression of this new tenant changed as the week progressed. When Manny didn't hand over a resume the next day, Irene was slightly concerned. Then it was one excuse after another to the point that Irene was having second thoughts about renting room 1B. Irene noticed that this new tenant would cover his face when passing the security cameras. Then she noticed an older lady going into his room.

What actually caused Irene to become suspicious of this new tenant was the fact that he seemed to be sneaking around the building and often appeared to be listening to her conversations on the phone. Several of her servants complained to her that they thought he was 'trouble.' Irene was convinced that Manny had to go. She explained to her accountant that she thought he was some type of drug dealer and she wanted him evicted even before the month was up.

Irene may have been feeling a certain degree of the distrust that was going around in 1998. The nation was in the thick of the Monica Lewinsky and President Bill Clinton extra-marital affair, which caused the President to be impeached by the House of Representatives. His famous quote for the year was "I did not have sexual relations with that woman . . . It depends on what the meaning of the word 'is' is."

Irene was repulsed with all the media hype about the affair since she was more concerned with what was happening on Broadway. She was excited that there was a new Swan Lake at the Neil Simon Theatre, which was set to open in October.

During this first week of July, Kenny continually tried to find out Irene's Social Security number. They were able to set up an eavesdropping device on Irene's phone line. He used all sorts of excuses to ask her staff personal information about her. However, he didn't realize how loyal her staff was since she treated them like part of her family. Sante and Kenny were intently gathering property transfer forms, including a deed of sale, which would be needed for the fraudulent transfer of the hotel. However, to complete the fraudulent transaction they needed Irene's Social Security number.

Sante and Kenny were professional scam artists and they took pride in how well they could forge a person's name. They were able to obtain documents with Irene's signature and they practiced for hours to learn how to copy it to perfection. When they were pleased with their forgeries they were ready for the next step, which was to find a notary.

Kenny was able to line up a notary to come over to his room 1B. When the notary arrived, Kenny had her come in and then had his mother, Sante, play the part of Irene Silverman. Sante prided herself as being a great actress. She was wearing a nightcap, and nightgown posing as a bedridden Irene Silverman. She pretended to sign the grant deed, and then Kenny wanted the notary to fix her seal over the signature. For some reason, the notary became suspicious and refused to notarize the document. Was it Sante's performance that was over the top, or had the notary seen the switching of the documents? The notary refused to notarize the document and walked out.

Kenny was concerned whether he could find a cooperative notary. For all those years in LA and Vegas, they were able to use Nannette Watson as their cooperative notary. At that moment in time, Kenny really missed having Watson available to help them to do their dirty work. On July 2nd, luckily Kenny rounded up another notary who came over to his room. Again Sante posed as an infirm Irene Silverman wearing a frilly nightgown and nightcap over a red wig. This second notary may have been in a hurry or overly impressed with the sizeable cash payment, in that she didn't seem too concerned to actually see Sante sign the document in front of her.

Sante and Kenny now had their sales agreements notarized, and the next step was to get someone to help them operate the hotel for a short time before they would sell it to someone for a price tag of eight to ten million dollars. Kenny contacted Stanley Peters, their old friend from Las Vegas. Stan lived in a tattered trailer park and eked out a living selling guns without asking too many questions. They promised to pay him well if he would fly from Las Vegas to New York and act as the manager of Irene Silverman's hotel. Stanley had held many questionable jobs and he had confidence that he could wing his way through this one.

The one reason that Kenny contacted Stan was that he could implicitly trust him. Stan had come to the aid of the Kimeses on many occasions. However, Stan didn't want to do prison time on something he didn't get anything out of. The police had been over to his place to ask about the transactions with the guns. The detectives also had spelled it out for Stan that they wanted Sante and Kenny Kimes. His transgressions on the gun deals could be easily overlooked if he would alert the detectives where the Kimeses might be found.

When Kenny called Stan to ask him to come to New York to help, Stanley had to feel he had been dealt a 'Free Jail Pass.' Kenny thought he was asking a favor from one of the family's most trusted friends. Unknown to Kenny was that his buddy was more interested in keeping his own ass out of jail than helping an old friend.

CHAPTER 36 DEATH OF IRENE SILVERMAN

Saturday, the fourth of July, 1998, in New York, was a big deal. This is the city with the Statue of Liberty, and it takes pride having a gigantic fireworks show in the New York harbor. For Irene the Fourth was a big occasion. She was the perfect example of what an American could achieve, since she had gone from rags to riches with some help from her late husband. Irene knew the hotel would be quiet this weekend, since most of her guests would be off on trips or vacation holidays. She had given most of the staff the weekend off.

Was Sunday morning, July 5, 1998, going to be a good day? The answer is whether you are a follower of the Church of the SubGenius, which holds that this is "X-Day," the day scheduled for "the end of the world." This group of people believed that an army of alien invaders would land on the planet Earth and destroy the world of "normals" while the church members are rescued by the aliens and taken away into space. The strange thing was in the past, July 5th came and went without the world coming to an end. However, this religious group still celebrated this day as being a Special day for them.

During the morning, around 11:00 a.m., Irene asked one of her remaining maids, Martha Rivera, to walk her dog on the roof garden. Her maid carried out her wish and took care of her dog. The hotel remained unusually quiet. Exactly what happened next is not known with certainty. However, the best inference from the facts is as follows: Sante and Kenny had everything in place to claim that they had purchased the Silverman's mansion and were going to take over the operation until they could find a buyer for this unique hotel. They had successfully obtained the notarizing of what appeared to be Irene Silverman's signature indicating the selling of the mansion to them. They had the money to pay the property transfer tax. Also, within several hours they would have a new manager for the hotel flying in from Las Vegas.

All that remained to complete their masterful fraud plan was to somehow dispose of Irene. What we don't know is whether Irene on her own went to room 1B to tell Manny (Kenny) that he was being evicted as of Monday or if Kenny went to Irene's office and asked her to come to his room so he could talk to her in private. What we do know is that Irene ended up in room 1B. Most likely there was an argument which led to a struggle. Irene was frail and elderly. She was no match for a tall male in his 20s with the help of a healthy female accomplice.

Unfortunately, Irene thought of herself as being invincible and was normally surrounded 24 hours a day by loyal staff members who would do anything to protect her. She most likely thought nothing bad could happen to her in her house where she had created a loving, caring atmosphere for everyone who stayed or lived there. Sante zapped Irene with a stun gun, which most likely paralyzed Irene's frail body.

Kenny grabbed Irene by the neck and he painstakingly strangled her. The process took a long time, and he had to continue to apply pressure to her neck. Because of her age the shock of it all may have killed her, but Kenny didn't let off the pressure until he was certain there was no more life left in Irene's body. As Irene's body dropped to the floor, Sante reached for the shower curtain they had purchased. She took the liner from the shower curtain and laid it on the floor and they rolled Irene's body up in it. In order for her body to stay wrapped tightly, Kenny took a roll of duct tape and started wrapping the tape around the ends of the shower liner. Two large trash bags were used to cover everything up.

Then Kenny rapidly walked down the hallway and out the front door without anyone seeing him. He went to the garage down the street where he had parked the Town Car. After waiting several minutes to retrieve the car, Kenny drove around the block and pulled up close to the front door of the hotel. Parking the car in a red zone was the only place he could find. Kenny immediately entered into the building and back to his apartment room 1B. They used a bedspread to cover the body in the shower liner then covered with trash bags. Kenny lifted Irene's body with the help of his mother and they commenced their criminal exit down the hall out the front door.

For both of them Irene's body felt like carrying dead weight, which it was. This was a strain on Sante and she didn't want to pull her back out of place. They approached the Lincoln in broad daylight. No one seemed to notice this mother-son team struggling to carry something long in trash bags. Since the trunk wasn't open the two of them gently placed the long wrapped item on the curb. Kenny got the key, pushed the button, and the trunk popped open. They both reached down and picked up the body and unceremoniously dropped it into the trunk.

As Kenny slammed the trunk lid closed he gave his mother a half grin. Sante wanted to say job well done but she knew there was much more to do to pull off the biggest fraud scam of her career, one which would be worth millions. So far, everything was going well. This Sunday morning was unusually serene compared to the usual hustle bustle of New York.

Sante reminded Kenny that he needed to return to the room and remove all his personal belongings. They felt secure now since the dead body was no longer in the room. They needed to collect all the paperwork and documents they had prepared as well as scraps of paper they had used to practice writing Irene Silverman's signature.

They decided to take all their personal belongings first and place them in the backseat of the car. After several trips to the Lincoln, they had well covered their tracks. Sante double checked the room and was satisfied they had removed all their personal items. As they say in the old Western movies, "Time to get out of Dodge."

On the following graphic page are photos of Sante and Kenny Kimes involved in killing Irene Silverman.

Graphics 15

KILLING OF IRENE SILVERMAN

Kill owner of this Brownstone Mansion so to get this property and later sell it for several million dollars.

This is reenactment from TV program showing how Irene Silverman was killed.

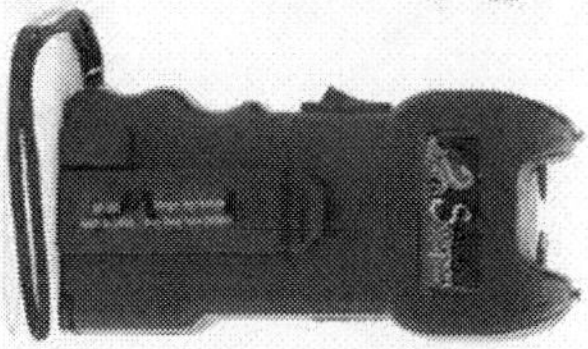

Sante used a stun gun on Irene while Kenny strangled her to death.

Arrested tin New York

Sante in Prison for
120 years to Life
Life without Parole

Kenny in Prison for
125 years to Life
Life without Parole

CHAPTER 37 DISPOSING OF THE BODY

To Kenny it seemed like deja vu. The entire incident of trying to get rid of the body reminded him of the time when he was in a rowboat and because of the heaviness of the dead body the boat got stuck on a sandbar. At that time, some police officers had come along and helped him off the sandbar so he could continue to row out to sea. Fortunately, this time no police officers came by or anyone offering to assist in lifting Irene's body into the trunk.

Sante and Kenny felt an enormous relief and realized that their great venture was running late. Both jumped in the Town Car and they turned on Madison Avenue and disappeared in a sea of yellow taxicabs. As they maneuvered through traffic, Kenny glanced around for signs pointing the way to the Holland Tunnel. When he found the entrance to the Tunnel he squeezed the battleship-size Town Car in the right lane. He pressed on the accelerator and the car lurched forward as they headed for the swamplands around Hoboken, New Jersey.

Over the years, Kenny had told his friends and associates that the family motto was, 'No Body, No Crime.' In order to stay true to the family motto, Kenny drove to a construction site in a desolate swampy area off of one of the New Jersey turnpikes.

Kenny was a master of making bodies disappear so that they were never found. He learned that from his mother, who had experienced it the hard way after serving several years in federal prison. With both Kenny and Sante instigating the plan, it is no wonder that even to this day Irene Silverman's body has never been found and she most likely is resting in peace wherever they dumped her body.

After Kenny and Sante had successfully disposed of Irene's body, they headed back to Manhattan. Since it was past 11:00 a.m., Kenny called the Hilton Hotel lobby and told them to inform Mr. Stan Peters (pseudonym) that they were having car trouble and would meet him later in the afternoon. Kenny dropped his mother off at the Plaza Hotel and looked for a nearby garage to park the car. Sante took a satchel and checked it in at the Plaza Hotel. It contained many of the documents regarding the transfer of Irene Silverman's property.

Both of them had had a stressful morning with the killing of Irene and disposing of her body. They knew they couldn't relax yet, since they had a busy afternoon in which they needed to be on their 'A Game' if they were to pull off such a sophisticated scam.

CHAPTER 38 LONG AFTERNOON

It was a little after 4:00 p.m. when the maid came by Irene's office and couldn't find her. She proceeded to Irene's apartment to see if she might have taken a nap and overslept. Martha Rivera became distressed, since Irene never ever went out of the hotel without one of the staff to accompany her. She checked with the cook and the one other worker and no one had seen or heard from Irene anytime during the afternoon.

By 5:00 p.m. the staff was alarmed and tried to determine where she could be. It wasn't long before the police were contacted and they responded to the hotel to obtain whatever information they needed for a Missing Persons Report. What the staff did find out was that the new tenant had moved out of apartment 1B. When they walked through that room, the staff noticed that a large pillow and comforter were missing from the bed. What was even stranger was that there was an opened roll of duct tape and a box of 42-gallon trash bags with four bags missing from the box. Furthermore, what didn't make any sense was the fact there was a shower curtain without its liner.

What did it all mean? Was there a connection no one knew? As the staff looked more at the office they noticed that the stacks of cash Irene kept in her office closet were also missing. The search was now on to find Irene.

Stanley Peters, who was the good friend of the Kimeses, had arrived in the Big Apple to meet with them. The police from the west coast wanted to arrest the Kimeses for the stealing of the Lincoln Town Car from a Utah dealer. LAPD was investigating the Kimeses for the murder of David Kazdin. The detectives encouraged Peters to fly to New York to meet the Kimeses. He was instructed to set up a meeting with them at the Hilton Hotel in New York. The police supplied him with a bulletproof vest and wired him for sound.

The meeting was set for 11:00 a.m. in the lobby of the Hilton Hotel. Federal agents of the fugitive task force were helping out the Utah Police in this arrest. No one knew that the mother- son team had just committed a murder of one of New York's most prominent citizens.

At the assigned time, Stanley Peters was waiting nervously for this meeting to occur. Neither Sante nor Kenny appeared. At 11:30 a.m. a phone call was received at the Hilton Hotel desk from the Kimeses explaining that they were having auto trouble and would be late. It wasn't until 5:00 p.m. that Sante appeared and sat down with Stanley and explained his duties as the new manager of the hotel. Not until 6:40 p.m. did Kenny arrive at the hotel after parking the Lincoln in a garage nearby, after which he went to meet with his mother and Stan in the lobby of the Hilton.

CHAPTER 39 ARREST AND SEARCH

The Hilton Hotel lobby was filled with people who had come to New York for the big Fourth celebration. Sante and Kenny were on the verge of pulling off the biggest scam of their lives. Stanley Peters didn't want the Kimeses to realize that he was double-crossing them big time. The fugitive officers knew that they were in a difficult environment to make an arrest of fugitives. The use of guns would definitely be highly problematic.

The officers noticed Kenny walking into the lobby and looking around for his mother and Stanley. The officers tried to approach Kenny without too much fanfare. But Kenny had spent most of his life running from the law. He had a sixth sense for recognizing cops. When the undercover officers came up on both sides of him, he sensed something was wrong. Kenny took off running like a deer in hunting season. A foot race ensued. The NYPD undercover officers knew where the exits were and they were able to cut Kenny off before he got out the door.

After Kenny had been apprehended, the other officers approached Sante, who was enjoying her conversation with their trusted friend Stanley. Sante looked up at the undercover officers wondering what was happening. She seemed confused that the officers were arresting her while her good friend seemed to be standing idly by. When the police had handcuffed both Sante and Kenny, that action ended one of the most notorious mother-son criminal careers. When the cops were leading Kenny away, they noticed that he had soiled his pants. Apparently this arrest had scared the crap out of Kenny.

The lead detective informed the two of them they were being arrested for Auto Theft of a Lincoln Town Car from a Utah dealer. A smile came over Kenny's face when he realized that the cops weren't aware of the murder of Irene Silverman. However, his smile faded as the officers started searching him and found the identification in the name of Manuel Guerrero and numerous documents in the name of Irene Silverman. He also had a knife and brass knuckles on his person. Also on Kenny's person was Irene Silverman's personal set of unique hotel keys. Kenny also possessed a black vinyl bag which contained more than $10,000 in cash and several documents bearing the name of Irene Silverman. They also found a parking stub for a nearby garage where they found the stolen Lincoln Town Car. It was towed over to the FBI headquarters, where it was searched pursuant to a search warrant.

When they searched the car they found documents in Irene's name, blank legal forms, notebooks, and other items, including a can of mace, handcuffs, a jar of sedatives, rubber gloves, 10 wigs in various colors, black garbage bags, an empty stun gun box, and a semi-automatic handgun with ammunition. They found documents of power-of-attorney forms, real estate transfer forms, and pieces of paper on which someone had been practicing Irene Silverman's signature, as well as $30,000 in cash. In the trunk was an empty duffel bag that was large enough to hold a body. Other items found were two rolls of duct tape, a shower liner, heavy duty garbage bags, and a clothesline.

The FBI fugitive unit was pleased that they were able to take into custody both Kimeses. They were coming up with all these items and documents with the name of Irene Silverman. None of the officers were aware of the Missing Person Report about Irene Silverman. However, the gods weren't looking down favorably on Sante and Kenny. One of the fugitive detectives just happened to glance at a TV set that was on. He heard the reporter mention the mysterious disappearance of an elderly socialite by the name of Irene Silverman and the authorities wanted to speak to a tenant at her hotel by the name of **Manny Guerrin**.

The detective thought that was the same name used by Kenny Kimes when he was arrested. That detective called the 19th Precinct and told the Inspector working the Missing Person case that they had the missing tenant in custody.

Then the FBI agent mentioned they had a lot of documents in the name of Irene Silverman, such as passports and a Social Security card. The Missing Person Inspector went over to talk to Sante, who was waiting to be booked on the fugitive Auto Theft Warrant. He asked her if she knew Irene Silverman, to which Sante denied knowing her and indicated that maybe she was out walking her dog. (This seemed to be a strange response if she really didn't know her.)

The satchel that Sante had taken to the **Plaza Hotel** contained considerable incriminating evidence. After Sante and Kenny were arrested, they hired an attorney to represent them. Their hope was to have the attorney get both of them out on a low bail before the police realized that Irene had been murdered. Sante told the attorney to have someone go to the Plaza Hotel and retrieve the satchel she had checked in. None of the detectives knew anything about it. The Kimeses' attorney hired a private investigator to go to the Plaza Hotel to pick up the satchel. The private investigator didn't have any difficulty retrieving the satchel and notifying the attorney. At that point, the attorney notified the police who obtained a search warrant for the satchel. (Apparently the attorney didn't want to become involved as an accessory after the fact to murder.)

After the satchel was seized, it was taken to the DA's Office, and in the presence of the Kimeses' defense attorney the satchel was opened and all the items were itemized for use in court. When they went through the satchel to inventory it, they found a treasure trove of items, including a loaded .22 caliber Beretta and numerous incriminating pieces of evidence that included a folder titled 'The Final Dynasty' which included the notarized deed, notarized transfer tax forms, and the other documents with the forged signature of Irene Silverman selling the hotel to Atlantis Group Ltd., a corporation set up by the Kimeses

CHAPTER 40 READY FOR NEW YORK TRIAL

The NYPD Police Commissioner described the Kimeses as "very competent, very violent, very cold criminals: the queen and prince of con artists." Mayor Rudolph Giuliani's Office offered an $11,000 reward and an exhaustive hunt for Irene Silverman's body began which included searching parks, rubbish dumps, and rivers. Investigators were called to a waste recycling center in the Bronx since one of the recycler employees had found a human leg and arm and wondered if it could belong to Irene Silverman. After a forensic examination, the parts were excluded as not belonging to Mrs. Silverman.

The trial of the Kimeses was heralded as the trial of the millennium. It was believed that the Kimes trial would likely be the most sensational and widely covered trial since that of O.J. Simpson. One newspaper heralded this case as one with no body and no direct evidence and was the type of case that will really tax the prosecutor's skills.

Just days before the big trial, both Sante and Kenny granted an interview to ***60 Minutes***. During the broadcast of the interview, Sante, who had turned 65 years old, and Kenny, who was then 25 years old, appeared stoic and confident they would be acquitted. They both explained, "There's no truth to any of this." Sante had on a gray oversized suit with her hair up, wearing stylish horn-rimmed glasses that gave her the image of a professional business woman. Throughout the interview, Sante clutched her dear son's hand as Kenny smiled wearing a black double-vested suit with a somber blue tie. Kenny gave the appearance of a happy mortician who was being overly protected by his dear mother.

It was hard to fathom the purpose of doing the ***60 Minutes*** interview. It did make this mother-son scam team look like human beings. However, the audience was informed about all the people who had been ripped off by the Kimeses or disappeared after meeting with them. A viewer might think of them as being a little too slick and slippery. Their rehearsed, polished answers only reinforced how good they were. There was the comparison with Bonny and Clyde, who traveled across the country wreaking havoc wherever they stopped. Some reporters were saying that they were the new 'Mommy and Clyde' team. As Sante held her head up high throughout the interview, she had to be thinking that she and her son had made it to the top. They were being admired for their accomplishments.

During the televised interview, their defense attorney, Mel Stein (pseudonym), was sitting off to the side of the pair. Reporter Steve Croft asked the question directed to Kenny, "Is it true that you took acting classes in college?" It might have been that they were looking so glib that their attorney rose up and told Sante and Kenny to terminate the interview. Sante gave her 'poor misunderstood look' to the camera as she took off her lavalier microphone. She hesitated on camera as though she still had important things to say. This was Sante's once-in-a-lifetime opportunity to shine on ***60 Minutes***. The entire nation could appreciate what an important person she had become. This was verification to her that she was the best of the best in her profession. Walking out in the middle of the interview had to be a giant disappointment for Sante, but she didn't question her attorney's motive for terminating the interview.

Within days, the New York trial began with Prosecutor Connie Fernandez saying in her Opening Statement to the jury, "They murdered Irene Silverman to get her out of the way. It's as simple as that . . . they used a stun gun to knock out Mrs. Silverman and then strangled her . . . they wrapped her body up and loaded it into the trunk of their car."

The prosecution wanted to establish that the Kimeses had a **Motive** to get rid of Irene. The way they established a motive to the jury was to show that the Kimeses wanted Silverman's place and that Irene would never willingly give up her hotel/house to them. Irene had planned to leave her place to a charitable foundation she had established in memory of her mother. The directors of the foundation would not personally benefit from Irene's death. However, the Kimeses would unquestionably benefit from her death. They had arranged for the transfer of her business and building to their 'shell corporation.' They could not assume full control of the property and reap the benefits of the house if Irene were still alive. The Kimeses knew that Irene would not allow them to take over the house so long as she was alive. Therefore, they had a strong motive to kill Irene.

Besides Motive, the Kimeses had the **Opportunity** as well as the means to kill Irene. Cell phone records showed that the Kimeses were in the mansion at the time of Irene's disappearance. The records show two calls made from their cell phone to the Plaza hotel. Those calls were made from inside the hotel or in the immediate vicinity of the hotel at 11:06 a.m. and 11:26 a.m. The only people in the hotel at that time were the Kimeses and Irene with her maid, Rivera, who was busy doing her chores. The Kimeses had the exclusive Opportunity to be present when Irene disappeared.

The Kimeses were also well equipped with **Tools to Murder** Irene Silverman. Various instruments that would assist in the murder and disposal of Irene were found in the Lincoln and the satchel that had been checked in at the Plaza Hotel. These instruments included two loaded guns, an empty stun gun box, drugs, syringes, large duffel bags, duct tape, and masks. Also found in room 1B were an open roll of duct tape bearing Kenny Kimes' prints, four heavy-duty garbage bags missing from a box of ten, and a shower curtain missing a plastic liner.

In order to answer the claim that there was no evidence of a struggle at the hotel, the prosecution argued that the Kimeses overpowered Irene Silverman without a struggle. The victim was 83 years old and at this time in her life she was four feet eight inches tall and weighing 115 pounds, compared to Kenny who was six feet tall and weighed 180 pounds and Sante who was five feet five inches tall and weighed 200 pounds. They could easily overpower Irene Silverman with sheer bodily force.

The prosecution showed the jury the **14 notebooks** that Sante kept containing minute details of the scheme, along with tape recordings they made of wiretaps they had placed on Irene's phone. These notebooks explained in Sante's words how they planned and carried out their various scams and murders. In Sante's handwriting were the words "Rich, elderly, easy marks." The notebooks listed the documents needed to transfer title of Irene's building and included a to-do list: get Silverman's Social Security number and examples of her signature, buy rope, stun gun, and gloves.

The prosecutors called a Ralph Pellas (pseudonym), an insurance salesman, to testify to the origin of the scheme to take Irene Silverman's hotel. It all started in 1996 when he and Sante were taking an anti-aging seminar in Las Vegas. He had met Mrs. Silverman and later told Sante how Silverman ran this unique hotel in New York in which she rented the rooms for up to $10,000 per month. Witness Pellas testified that Sante was extremely interested that this widow owned this property outright without any mortgage. She wanted more information and he told her that she could use the name Rudy Vaccari as a reference.

Then the prosecutors called members of Silverman's staff, who testified that two months before the disappearance of Mrs. Silverman, a woman called about renting a room and used the reference of Rudy Vaccari.

CHAPTER 41 STRANGE DEFENSE

The Defense claimed that there was no forensic evidence connecting the Kimeses to the alleged murder. They explained it was a case based on speculation and misinformation. There wasn't a body, there were no eyewitness accounts, no fingerprints, no hair, no blood or fibers to link them to the victim. On top of all that, there was no confession or admissions to be introduced by the prosecution. The evidence was entirely circumstantial. The Defense claimed that "There are other individuals who would have benefited from Ms. Silverman's death, such as people who had an interest in the property who were beneficiaries in her will. Further, there was dissension between her and some business associates. She'd made enemies, and the prosecutor should be investigating those people because we, the Defense, certainly have."

During the trial the judge ordered the mother and son to stop holding hands in front of the jury. Further, the judge ordered the Kimeses not to speak to the news media. But Sante couldn't restrain herself and was caught passing a note to a reporter. The judge threatened to have Sante handcuffed during further proceedings if she continued to contact the media. The judge restricted Sante's phone access to only her attorneys. The judge sustained a motion that Sante was attempting to influence the jury since they might hear stories about the case through the news media.

The judge had ruled that her prior slavery conviction could be used to impeach Sante if she decided to testify. Since the defense attorneys didn't want the jury to hear about her prior conviction, Sante had chosen not to take the witness stand.

The prosecutor in her final Argument said, "Do not reward these defendants because they were clever enough to dispose of the victim's body."

After the 15-week trial involving the testimony of 130 witnesses and 430 exhibits, the jury, comprising eight women and four men, deliberated for four days. When the jury buzzed that they had reached a verdict, Sante and Kenny were brought into the courtroom and sat at the counsel table. They were apathetic and listened to the guilty verdicts, which took 20 minutes for the forewoman to read. Partway through the reading Kenny leaned over to his mother and whispered, "Mom, it'll be OK."

They were found guilty of multiple counts of murder in the second degree, robbery and burglary in the first degree, criminal possession of a weapon in the second and third degree, 16 counts of forgery in the second degree, criminal possession of a forged instrument in the second degree, 29 counts of eavesdropping, criminal possession of stolen property in the third degree, conspiracy in the fourth degree, and attempted grand larceny in the first degree.

Later, at the time of sentencing, the judge gave Sante an opportunity to make a statement. Sante seemed like a clock wound too tight. She sprang forth with a mouth full of words that few courtrooms have ever heard. Her statement pointed the blame to authorities, including her lawyers, all of those who had framed her. She continued on to compare their trial to the 'Salem Witch Trials' and indicated that the prosecutors were guilty of 'Murdering the Constitution.' Then it was the opportunity for the judge to express her opinion about Sante. The judge said that Mrs. Kimes was "a sociopath and a degenerate" and her son was duped and "a remorseless predator." Then the judge imposed the sentence of 120 years in prison for Sante, while Kenny received slightly more with a sentence of 125 years in prison.

Sadly Sante said in a dejected voice to her attorney, "What's next? Is this the end of everything for us?" But an hour later Sante was in better spirits as the TV cameras were focused on her, and in a strong defiant voice she said, "The verdict is an insult to justice and a temporary setback."

In March of 2001, Sante and Kenny agreed to do separate interviews with the ***Larry King TV Show***. This interview was very revealing to the public as to Sante's thought process and insight on how a sociopath explains her actions. At the time, Larry King's CNN TV program was the way the USA TV audience learned about celebrities, politicians, and important events. Being invited to appear on the Larry King show was more advantageous than their failed attempt on ***60 Minutes.*** Here, Sante would have a forum to profess their innocence. She was confident that she could easily handle any questions fielded by Larry King.

Sante and Kenny were going to have the opportunity to tell the world their story. They wanted to be sure the public was interested in hearing from them since neither of them took the witness stand. The public did have some idea what their side of the story could be. For Sante and Kenny, this was the perfect opportunity to tell their version without having a prosecutor unmercifully cross-examine them. They had no idea how well prepared Larry King would be in his questioning. Larry was often accused of playing softball and merely throwing gentle questions to his guests, who could then belt them out of the park. What was going to be Sante's approach? Could she answer the questions without incriminating herself?

The following are excerpts from the transcript of Larry King's Interview:

SANTE KIMES: I don't think there are words where I could really tell you, but I know justice is coming, and I know that the world is going to help us bring out justice . . . So I tried to feel that even though it wasn't so unjust, that there is a light, and the truth is coming.

LARRY KING: So you feel your appeals are going to work?

SANTE KIMES: They have to, or there is not any justice left in the country, Larry.

LARRY KING: The biggest injustice is obviously you say, you didn't do it.

SANTE KIMES: The biggest injustice is that there is no crime. They don't know where the woman is. They manufactured a crime. What happened is, I'm sure that the world knows, that New York is one of the most corrupt law systems in the world. Last week in the papers they were monitoring now . . .

LARRY KING: In a missing person, you suspect a crime don't you? And I mean if you were a police officer and someone is missing and you don't find them, you suspect someone did something to them . . .

SANTE KIMES: You'd suspect, and I'm glad you asked that, because then you'd find evidence, and there is no evidence. They have no evidence. They have no body, no reliable evidence, and no witnesses.

LARRY KING: Weren't cards found on you and your son that belonged to her?

SANTE KIMES: No.

LARRY KING: Then how did they connect the two?

SANTE KIMES: All of those things and what I was going to ask you, please, and ask the world, people who believe in justice, before we couldn't get our teeth into anything and prove what was being done, but after we lost in the lower trial. Now things are on the record, and if agencies or people who believe in justice will just read the transcript, they'll see exactly what happened. They don't have to – you don't have to believe us.

The interview started off with Sante claiming that she was begging for justice since she and her son were convicted in a 'No Body' case in which she claimed there was no evidence. She sounded like she was restating the family motto, which was 'No Body, No Crime.' She was trying to spin the discussion from all the evidence they were caught with to the argument the New York police were corrupt and out to get them.

The next part of the interview shows how Sante can tell bald-faced lies to the TV audience without any hesitation and with a straight face. Larry tries to pin her down as to her and Kenny renting the room from Irene Silverman. It's like Sante was trying to say black is white and white is black. As to them renting the room, there were numerous witnesses who saw Kenny rent the room and live there for several weeks. This part of the interview illustrates how Sante could turn anything upside down. Here she talks about meeting Irene Silverman and dealing with her and the apartment when, in fact, she had purposely gone out of her way to avoid meeting her.

LARRY KING: You rented the apartment?

SANTE KIMES: No, but I talked about it. We became kind of social friends. I didn't see her again until she called me in 1996 and told me that she was worried, and that she wanted to sell her apartment, that she had a lot of people around her talking her into willing it to them, that she didn't—had changed her mind. She wanted to sell it. And she knew that, you know, I had a lot of connections and I could help her, and I said I'd be happy to . That's how it all started.

LARRY KING: Did you eventually rent it or buy it?

SANTE KIMES: No, No.

LARRY KING: Your son lived there?

SANTE KIMES: Not at all.

LARRY KING: You had no connection with that apartment at all, other than trying to help her?

SANTE KIMES: Listen, all we did—that apartment, police have totally—they haven't even told the public that we didn't even rent the apartment. We did not even rent the apartment.

In the next part of the interview Larry King asked about all the items found on the Kimeses and in their car. It would seem that most people would try to give some reason for having the various items. But Sante uses the approach that they didn't have any of the items and that they were all planted on them by the police.

SANTE KIMES: OK. I'm glad you asked me this question. If you read the transcripts, if everybody, anyone who believes in justice will . . . you will see that this was all planted. The police on the stand . . . admitted that there was no trail of evidence. They had not . . . all of that was planted on us.

LARRY KING: They came to plant this evidence on you?

SANTE KIMES: We didn't have any any . . . Larry, we didn't have any keys.

LARRY KING: Or guns, or syringes or anything.

SANTE KIMES: No

LARRY KING: Why you?

SANTE KIMES: Because we were there, and because the people did not want her to sell that apartment, I guess, because there was an arrest over a little car thing. A bookkeeper had written a check, and it bounced on a car deal, and they held us, and then we went into this.

LARRY KING: The police set you up?

SANTE KIMES: Like they admitted it on—if you will read the transcripts, you will see that there is no trail of evidence. The police admit it, that they didn't voucher anything. Kenny didn't have any keys on him. I didn't have any passports. None of her things were on us. They went in the apartment the day of the disappearance, and they got all that stuff, and it was planted.

Defendants often will use the police planting argument as to one or two items, but Sante was bold enough to do it as to everything that was found on them and the car. It was interesting how Sante describes the theft of the Lincoln Town Car as an arrest over 'a little car thing.'

The interview took another peculiar turn when Larry King asked Sante about why the judge described her as "the most degenerate defendant who had ever appeared in her courtroom." Then Sante showed the paranoid side of herself. There was no remorse but 'Poor Me.'

SANTE KIMES: I think that New York is one of the most corrupt political systems in the world, they're being federally monitored . . .

LARRY KING: So the judge could say, OK, this is a terrible woman, why say the most degenerate defendant ever?

SANTE KIMES: Well, you know, it not only blew me away. A fair judge would not say that. I mean, a judge is not supposed to talk like that. They're supposed to be unbiased. Do you know that judge, Uviller, that judge told the jury when it first started, if you think that you have to have a body here, you know, then you don't belong on this jury. That judge stopped me from taking the stand.

LARRY KING: I'm talking about in the trial, why didn't you take the stand?

SANTE KIMES: I begged. She stopped me from even talking to Mel, my attorney, the other attorneys. She stopped me, and I wanted to take the stand. I begged to be able to even talk to my attorneys . . .

LARRY KING: What about your son?

SANTE KIMES: Same thing.

LARRY KING: They wouldn't let him take the stand?

SANTE KIMES: No, he wasn't going to take the stand, but I wanted to, but everything she ruled . . . So we didn't really have any strategy or defense from May 5th until May 18th, the trial ended and we had a defense. We were ready to tell a brainwashed jury what happened, like where we think the woman is, that there was a legitimate sale. The judge, to me, is really the worst, the worst guilty person in all of this.

Sometimes it is hard to follow Sante's message. She blamed the judge for most of her problems. What she wasn't telling Larry was the fact that her Slave Trade conviction was going to be revealed to the jury if she took the witness stand. Both sides can bring out the fact that a witness had been convicted of a felony. The judge had ruled that if Sante took the witness stand the prosecutor could impeach her testimony by the fact that she was a convicted felon. Sante wanted the jury to be sympathetic to her and she didn't want the jury to know about her criminal history.

During the trial, Sante was trying to keep her past stuffed in an invisible closet for no one to see. The news media had painted her not only to be a fraud but she could have won the worst mother of the year award. It was interesting how Larry and Sante danced around the incestuous relationships.

LARRY KING: What do you make of the stories that have appeared about you and your son? Because that has added to the spice of this case, that you had some sort of incestuous relationship.

SANTE KIMES: When I first heard this, I thought, you know, I thought of all the slime that they could go into, but I guess I didn't realize, you know, how far they can sink. They – my son, I held on my heart when he was born. He slept with my husband and I. That is ridiculous. It is so slimy and so ridiculous that I don't even have to answer it.

LARRY KING: You've never had relationships with him.

SANTE KIMES: No, my relationship with my son is he is a handsome wonderful kid that loves girls. He is a wonderful son. I'm proud of him. And he is going through hell on earth, hell on earth.

The interview was lengthy but gave Sante what she wanted more than anything else, a chance to commit the biggest fraud of all. Throughout her whole life she was trying to persuade people that whatever she was doing or selling was the truth. Could she con the world? She had just been sentenced to 120 years in prison, which might depress most people and even make them contrite. But not for Sante, she wasn't about to demonstrate any remorse or change her evil ways. She was about to be shipped to California, where she could still be sentenced to the Death Penalty.

CHAPTER 42 FROM NEW YORK TO CALIFORNIA

Shortly after the verdict and sentencing, Kenny's life took on another bizarre turn. He was doing an interview in prison with a freelance Court TV reporter when he took her hostage by grabbing a ballpoint pen and placing it against her throat. He told authorities he would stab her if they didn't comply with his demands. After three hours of negotiations with Kenny, he finally dropped the pen. As a result of this incident, Kenny was given eight years in solitary confinement for the hostage-taking.

It was extraordinary that Larry King was willing to do an interview with Kenny, but apparently they took all the ballpoint pens away from him. Undoubtedly, security was tight when the CNN TV interview occurred. Kenny was even smoother than his mother. He could take any question from Larry and spin it into whatever he wanted to complain about. Larry asked Kenny why he and his mother were convicted. He laid the blame on the fact that the investigators didn't take any notes for the last two years. His other excuse was that there was a photo that showed a possible security camera viewing of the front of Irene's hotel and its film was never seized and examined by the police. Kenny took the lack of notes and non-seizure of the camera to illustrate how the police and DA were out to get Kenny and his mother.

KENNY KIMES: Which tells me, no notes over two years. And if they wanted us, and if they wanted to prove our guilt, they would have taken the film and they would have used that camera as an aspect of their leading evidence in the case . . . They could take the camera out, and they did it intentionally.

LARRY KING: And why do they want to get you, so you think? New York City police don't know you.

KENNY KIMES: I think we're the easy whipping boy.

LARRY KING: Why would you be whipping boy when someone is just missing?

KENNY KIMES: It's an election year. Publicity, negative publicity, the public loves it. We're selling papers, clearly . . . But why me? Because I'm easy. I'm a foreigner, I'm out of town. They can just point the finger at the out-of-towners. There's always been an easy ability for people to just pick on someone who's not the local.

Kenny was good at playing the 'Minority Card' that he was treated unfairly since he was an outsider. But when Larry asked why he didn't testify, Kenny gave an incredible response.

KENNY KIMES: Why didn't I testify? Because I thought my mom was going to have a shot at testifying on her own.

LARRY KING: But when she didn't, why didn't you?

KENNY KIMES: Well, why didn't I? I figured at the beginning, we wanted to get Court TV to come in. I figured, if this judge isn't going to let Court TV come in, and is only going to allow a one-sided print media to get only what the DA feeds them, I might as well be careful and stand guard knowing what kind of unfairness is going to take place.

LARRY KING: Even though the jury would have the ability to see you.

KENNY KIMES: Never. It was too late. At that point, there was not a chance.

It is difficult to follow Kenny's reasoning that the fact that Court TV was excluded meant he couldn't or wouldn't be able to testify. But he did give an answer that some people might take under consideration. Next, Larry asked directly if they were involved in Irene Silverman's disappearance. Kenny answered unequivocally that they had nothing to do with the crime.

KENNY KIMES: Well. Larry, I did not do this. I did not commit this crime. I was arrested at the Hilton. There are no eyewitnesses. There was no physical evidence. I have no motive to commit this.

LARRY KING: I'm trying to figure out your motive?

KENNY KIMES: They said that we wanted to rob the house. They said we wanted to steal the mansion. For the love of God, how do you steal a mansion? How do you steal a mansion?

LARRY KING: Do you believe she's dead?

KENNY KIMES: This woman? Honestly? I have no idea. And for me to speculate would make me as bad as the jury who speculated upon us.

Some people look at any defendant charged with a crime as the underdog and in some way may want to believe the person is innocent. Undoubtedly, some readers may feel sorry for Kenny since he so adamantly claimed that he had nothing to do with Silverman's death. Maybe he is telling the truth. For those readers who believed him, the next paragraphs may be disconcerting.

Only a short time after the Larry King interview, Kenny was showing authorities where Irene's body was buried. He did this so the authorities would reduce the amount of time he had to spend in solitary confinement. Kenny's change of heart shocked his attorney, since now he admitted he had been involved in the victim's death. This would wipe out his claim on appeal that he was an innocent person who was unfairly convicted. Kenny was having a 'reality check' since now he accepted the fact that he was going to spend the rest of his life in prison. As a professional schemer, why not make it as pleasant as possible for one's self? Solitary confinement was not the way he wanted to spend the next eight years of his life.

What Kenny told law enforcement was, "I packaged Mrs. Silverman's body . . . placed it in the trunk of the car, and drove through the Holland Tunnel. I dumped her body at a New Jersey construction site 35 to 40 minutes from Manhattan."

In New York, Kenny had been sentenced to 125 years to life and Sante had been sentenced to 120 years to life. The question becomes what is enough of a sentence. Some people would say that was enough since Sante wouldn't come up for a parole hearing until 2119. Would California want to bring them back for the murder of David Kazdin? The Los Angeles County District Attorney's Office had to make the determination. One of the advantages that Los Angeles DA's Office had was that it had a knowledgeable Extradition Unit. (One of the duties of the author was to supervise the DA's Extradition Unit). This Unit, at any one time, has hundreds of extradition cases it is pursuing in the other 49 states and dozens of foreign countries. One of the advantages of the LA DA's Office is that it has incredible patience. Some extraditions will take years and sometimes require special documents to be translated into various foreign languages.

One of the classic statements made by Sante, when she was in court waiting for the extradition hearing, was "When is this all going to end?" Apparently Sante was tired of court proceedings. What she didn't realize was that the Los Angeles DA's Office wanted defendants to be accountable. Many jurisdictions don't have the experience or resources as does the LA District Attorney's Office, and the smaller

DA's Offices will refuse to spend the time and resources to extradite many of their fugitives.

When the LA DA's Office heard about the arrest of Sante and Kenny in New York, they set in motion the extradition request for both of them. California has the Death Penalty on the books while New York does not have such a law. This fact created an interesting issue. Should California have the opportunity to try the Kimeses first, since they could impose the Death Penalty in California? The LA DA's Office felt it should and sent their extradition request to California's Governor, at the time Gray Davis. The Governor's Office then submitted the application to the New York's Governor George E. Pataki. This required considerable bureaucratic paperwork that had to contain the approved extradition documents with the governor's seals affixed to them.

Although the extradition documents are impressive with all their seals and ribbons, the process is quite different from other legal proceedings. In extradition hearings, the state and federal law requires that a court hearing be held as in this case, in New York, at which time the defendants can waive their rights or oppose the extradition request. Extradition hearings are limited to determining whether or not the person named in the extradition request is the person in custody. Also, whether the offense of which they are accused is a crime and whether the defendant was in the requesting state at the time of the offense charged and fled it to avoid prosecution. How this hearing is different from other criminal proceedings is that the burden is on the defendant to disprove these issues. No evidence is permitted on the strength of the requesting state's case or the guilt or innocence of the defendant.

Governor Pataki approved the extradition and stated, "These murderers must be held accountable for each and every one of their vile acts." He agreed the Kimeses could be extradited to Los Angeles at the completion of all proceeding in New York. In other words, California would get them but New York wanted to try them first.

CHAPTER 43 SANTE'S TRIAL IN LOS ANGELES

In May of 2002, the Los Angeles Grand Jury indicted Sante and Kenny Kimes, charging them with the murder of David Kazdin. A special circumstance allegation of financial gain was added to the murder charge.

On November 17, 2003, Kenny was brought into the Los Angeles courtroom of Judge Kathleen Kennedy-Powell. Kenny's attorney stated to the court that Kenny was willing to plead guilty to the charge of murder of David Kazdin. The prosecutor, Eleanor Hunter, in open court stated that the prosecution would **not** seek the Death Penalty against Kenny Kimes. The prosecutor then asked him, "In this case, Kenneth Kimes Jr., how do you plead to the murder of David Kazdin?" Kenny, with a contrite soft voice, uttered the word **"GUILTY."**

In order to get a factual basis for the plea, Ms. Hunter asked Kenny if he had been to Kazdin's home on March 19, 1998, and shot David Kazdin. Kenny very calmly and resolutely said, "Yes." He further admitted disposing of the body in order to conceal a fraud committed against the victim. The prosecutor indicated that this plea was based on the fact that Kenny Kimes had agreed to testify against his 64-year-old mother.

Later that day, Sante Kimes appeared in the same court with her attorney Charles Maple. She pled **Not Guilty** and the matter was set for trial. She played the sympathy card throughout her many court appearances, including arriving via wheelchair, having fainting spells, claiming she was having a heart attack, and always uncontrollably weeping.

Sante's trial began on June 14, 2004, with the prosecutor, Eleanor Hunter, stating to the jury in her Opening Statement, "Kenny was Sante's enforcer, the one she would send to do all her dirty work." Sante's defense attorney said, "Sante cannot accept that her son would commit such a violent crime. My client did not order any killing and there was no motive for her to want Kazdin dead. It had nothing to do with Mrs. Kimes."

This type of case is one of the most challenging for a prosecutor to try in front of a jury. By needing to use an accomplice's (Kenny's) testimony, the prosecutor had to corroborate Kenny's testimony with other witnesses. In this case, the key witness was one of the biggest scam artists in the country. The prosecutor was trying to prove to the jurors that this time he was being truthful. Kenny Kimes most likely has told more lies than just about anyone else. So how do you know when he is telling the truth? On June 17 he took the witness stand and the court clerk asked him to swear to tell the truth and nothing but the truth. He resolutely responded that he would, then he testified that his mother said to him, "We're going to have to kill him." He went on to say that his mother had planned the murder on March 13, 1998, after Kazdin discovered the loan and refused to say to the bank he had authorized it. Kenny said that his mother said to him, "She wished me luck and told me to do a good job."

Kenny related to the jury that he and an accomplice, Sonny Lane, went to Kazdin's house that morning with trash bags, a .22-caliber gun, gloves, and duct tape. He indicated that he confronted Kazdin about the loan and Kazdin told him not to worry. Then Kenny followed him into the kitchen and he took out the gun. He testified, "I shot him in the back of the head at point-blank range to minimize the risk of error." Then he and Sonny Lane cleaned up the crime scene and threw Kazdin's body in the trunk of his Jaguar and drove to an area near LAX, covered the body with trash bags, and left it in a trash dumpster. Also, they threw out the gun and Kazdin's wallet a short distance away in another dumpster.

Kenny explained to the jury what they did next. "We ate lunch and went to see the movie, 'The Man in the Iron Mask', and shopped for clothes. Then after dark we returned to the airport area and disposed of the body. Afterward we headed to the Valley, where I stopped to buy some flowers." When asked by the prosecutor what he did with the flowers he said, "I kissed my mother and handed her the flowers and told her everything was OK." When asked why he did that he said, "In my mindset, I thought I had completed a great duty for my mom. It was a significant completion and I wanted to celebrate."

The following graphic shows how defiant Sante was all the way to the end.

Graphics 16

SANTE KIMES CASE IN LOS ANGELES

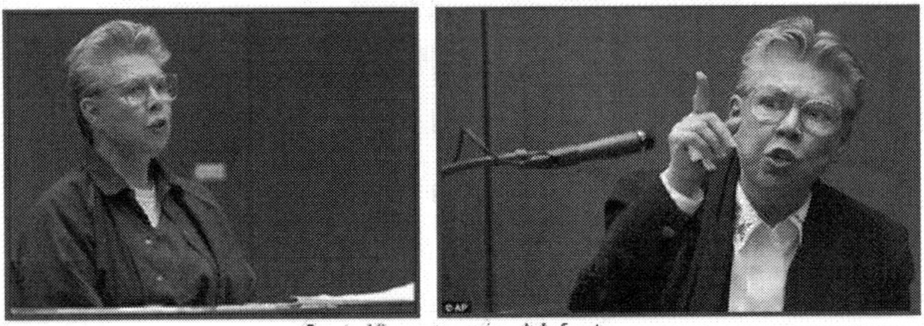

Sante Kimes remained defiant.

In prison interview Kenney placed pen against reporters neck.
In order to get out of isolation cell he agreed to testify against mother.

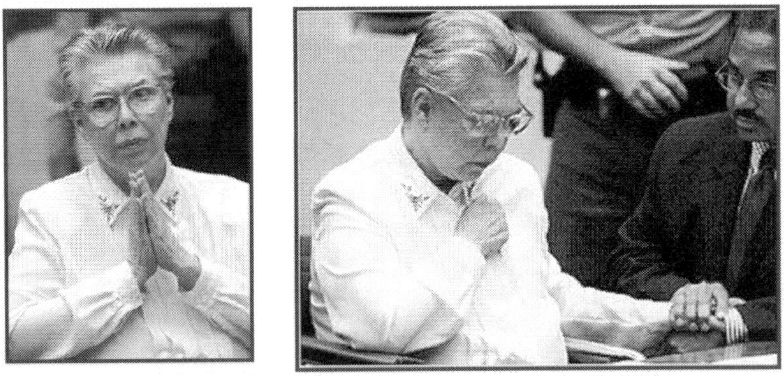

Sante continued to the end to give excuses for her behavior.

CHAPTER 44 OTHER PROSECUTION WITNESSES

Sonny Lane was unavailable to testify in court, but he had testified at the Grand Jury and the parties stipulated that the transcript of his testimony could be read in court.

Nannette Watson testified next that she met Sante in 1993 and she was hired as a part-time bookkeeper and worked at the Geronimo Way residence. Sante encouraged her to become a notary. Over a period of weeks, she saw McDonald do maintenance work around the house. He was given a room to stay in and was strictly not permitted to leave the house.

Sante instructed her to sign and notarize Kazdin's name on the loan documents, including the quitclaim deed and a deed of trust. The notary claimed that Sante said she had a power of attorney for Kazdin. Sante used Watson's bank account much like her own without the Kimeses' name on it. When the bank loan was funded, the money was placed in Watson's bank account and later she wired $120,000 to a bank account in Florida that the Kimeses used.

Later, Sante and Kenny had her join them on a so-called shopping trip to Los Angeles, where she was to meet with Kazdin. She went to his house while the Kimeses waited in their car down the street. She knocked on the door and Kazdin's daughter let her in. She talked to him about her problem with the bank, which he claimed he didn't know anything about. Then she left and went back to the car and met with the Kimeses.

She further testified that Kenny wanted her notary book, which she gave to him. He immediately destroyed it. Months later, **after the Kimeses were arrested in New York,** Watson received a letter from Sante which urged her **not** to talk about the Kazdin transaction, explaining that Kazdin had authorized her to sign his name. Sante wrote in the letter, "If DK (David Kazdin) is really gone, we certainly can't be connected to that. David is the only one who could at this time say he didn't sign papers or tell you to notarize." Nannette Watson was able to explain how the property was transferred by using forgeries. The next witness was the person that the property was supposedly transferred to.

Robert McDonald was the next witness the prosecutor called to the witness stand to relate his role in the property scam. He stated that he met Sante on November 8, 1996, when he was a homeless person. He agreed to work as the Kimeses' maintenance person and they would provide him room and board. They took his identification and ordered him not to leave the house. They cashed his Social Security checks and seldom gave him any of the money.

For whatever reason, they used his name on a quitclaim deed, purportedly signed by a David Kazdin, conveying the Geronimo Way property to him for the full sum of $10. Also, they used his name on a fire insurance policy on the house without his knowledge.

McDonald went on to testify that he helped Kenny move some furniture out of the house. He explained they moved into a duplex to live in on the other side of Las Vegas. Later, he traveled with the Kimeses to Los Angeles and stayed at a motel. While there they told him that the Geronimo Way house had burnt down because of an electrical fire. When they returned to Las Vegas to live in the duplex, he was told that the title to the Geronimo Way property was put in his name because of some legal problems they were having.

He related that they wanted him to meet with a fire insurance company investigator to answer certain questions about the $500,000 fire loss. He did his best at the meeting, claiming that he was the owner of the house that burned. After the meeting, he returned to a place in Bel Air where they were all staying. He was ordered not to tell anyone who they were or what they were up to. However, he told another tenant who the Kimeses really were and what they were planning to do. As a result, he described to the jury how Kenny and Sante beat him up for talking to the other tenants.

Further, McDonald related that one day he overheard Sante tell Kenny, "He knows too much. We have got to do something about him." Kenny replied, "What about his daughter?" Sante responded, "She won't be any problem." A few days later, Kenny and Sonny Lane left the Bel Air house early in the morning. They returned later that night and Kenny gave his mother a bouquet of flowers and kissed her. On the next day the landlord came by and that was when Kenny went ballistic and they all moved out. They all went to a restaurant to regroup, and that was when McDonald ran away, never to return to the Kimeses.

Attorney **Allen Rucker** testified that he worked at a company called Nevada Corporate Services. He worked as a resident agent for Nevada corporations, and Sante wanted his help to bring her Agahan corporation out of default. The main asset of the corporation was the Santa Maria property that was tied up in the civil lawsuit. Later in 1998, she wanted David Kazdin to be made an officer of the corporation. He claimed that he was contacted by phone by a person claiming to be Kazdin and he consented to be added as an officer.

Sante later asked him to take out a loan on the Geronimo Way residence; however, he needed Kazdin's consent since his name was on the land title. Sante assured him that the property was really hers so Kazdin would be no problem. Rucker never contacted him to obtain his consent, but when he received the loan documents, they had Kazdin's signature on them. When the loan money was paid, part of it went to Sante's offshore bank accounts. It was not until February 1998 that he became aware that Kazdin denied signing the loan, at which point Rucker said he terminated his relationship with the Kimeses.

To continue with the loan testimony, **Brenda Roberts** (pseudonym) was called as the next witness. She testified she worked for OCWEN Financial Services and she was the one who received the loan documents for the property on Geronimo Way. She had Kazdin's signature on the quitclaim deed that transferred the property to McDonald (which was notarized by Watson). The loan amount of $280,000 was funded and part of the money was wired to Watson's account. There was a request by the loan applicant (Sante Kimes) that **all correspondence be sent to the Geronimo Way address.** Unfortunately the bank made a mistake and **sent a billing statement and payment book to Kazdin's residence**.

That clerical error ended up to be a deadly mistake since that prompted Kazdin to call the finance company. She related that Kazdin was upset that he had been sent the material in error. He claimed that he didn't sign any loan application and indicated that the loan was a fraud. Since she had distributed most of the funds to a Nannette Watson's bank account, she immediately placed a hold on any remaining funds to be distributed.

Clifford Mitchell, an expert in arson detection, testified that he investigated the Geronimo Way property fire on January 31, 1998, and found it was intentionally set. He testified that he was able to locate several points on the floor where accelerant had been poured. As he examined the remains of the house, he determined that there was no evidence of an electrical or gas fire.

Stanley Peters testified that he helped the Kimeses do some furniture moving. Then Kenny asked him if he could obtain several handguns. This witness said he could provide Kenny with any kind of handgun he needed for $1,000. Eventually he returned to Los Angeles and brought Kenny a .22 Jennings handgun along with two other handguns and gave them to Kenny. After the shooting, he drove the Kimeses' RV from Las Vegas to a restaurant in LA where they all met.

The testimony then turned to the victim, David Kazdin. **Phillip Eaton** (pseudonym) testified that he was a longtime friend and attorney of David Kazdin. Kazdin had told him that his name was used on the title of the Geronimo Way property to help out his old friend, Kenneth Kimes Senior. Kazdin had asked that his name be removed from the title of the property, but it was never removed. Kazdin told him that in 1998 there was an unauthorized loan on that property using his name. Kazdin told him that he had not signed a quitclaim deed in favor of McDonald.

Further evidence about the victim continued with **Linda Kazdin** being called as a witness and testifying that she was the daughter of the victim. She noticed something was wrong when she went to her father's home and saw that his bed was unmade and his shoes were beside it. Also, his car was gone and the answering machine was blinking with more than 10 messages.

Daniella Swanson (pseudonym) testified that she lived on El Vido Drive in Bel Air and the Kimeses were renting rooms there. In their room was a map to Kazdin's house that they had apparently left behind.

Officer **Dale Best** of LAPD testified he was the officer who was sent to check out a dumpster with a body in it. He verified that the dumpster did contain a body covered by black plastic trash bags. The body didn't contain any wallet or identification. The victim's Jaguar was found about a mile away, parked in a shopping center parking lot.

Finally, the prosecutor addressed the issue of the cause of death. **Dr. Irwin Golden** was called to the witness stand as the medical examiner, and he testified that he performed the autopsy on David Kazdin. He was able to determine that the victim had been killed by a single gunshot wound to the back of the neck at the base of the skull. The gun had been fired from very close range. A small-caliber bullet was recovered from the victim's jaw.

CHAPTER 45 INTERESTING DEFENSE

James Burns (pseudonym), an attorney for the victim Kazdin, testified that Kazdin contacted him when he discovered the loan fraud. He did state that Kenny was a loose cannon. The Defense wanted to discredit Kenny in the eyes of the jury. When this witness was cross-examined, he indicated that Sante had threatened Kazdin and left threats on his voicemail.

Allen Glass was not a lengthy witness since he only testified that he was the one who was instrumental in obtaining the loan on the Geronimo Way property. With all of his contacts, he was able to find the best loan rates from a bank in Florida, which was OCWEN Bank.

The head LAPD investigator on the case was **Detective English**. It seemed unusual when the Defense called him to testify for them. They asked him whether witness James Burns had said that Kenny was a loose cannon. The detective related that Burns had said something to that effect. Everyone in the courtroom was befuddled as to what that had to do with the killing of Kazdin.

Against her attorney's advice, **Sante Kimes** eagerly wanted to testify. She emphatically told the jury that she had absolutely nothing to do with Kazdin's murder. She related how fond she was of David Kazdin and how much she loved him more than anyone in the world, except for her husband. On cross–examination the prosecutor asked her if she had been convicted of a felony. She denied any conviction. When she was asked specifically about the five federal felony convictions for slavery in 1985, she said that she didn't consider herself to have been guilty of those offenses. The prosecutor asked if those convictions involved five young women she had brought to Las Vegas from Mexico who testified that she physically abused them. She adamantly denied there was any abuse.

When asked about the murder of Syed Ahmed she denied any involvement. But when asked about her convictions in the Irene Silverman case she indicated she was wrongfully convicted and she insisted that she was truly good friends with Irene Silverman. When she denied the murder and offered an alibi, the prosecutor asked her whether she had any of Silverman's property in her possession at the time of her arrest. Sante thought for a moment about Irene's passports and Social Security card she had and said to the prosecutor, "I don't remember."

She spent much of three hours on the witness stand either crying or bawling. She accused a detective of planting evidence and called the prosecutor a monster and launched into several diatribes that prompted the judge to tell her to be quiet. Then Sante referred to Kazdin and said, "God bless him, wherever he is, I wish he were here to help me, I need help." She went on to say that she had been to his Granada Hills home more than 200 times and that neither she nor her son had anything to do with his death. She blamed his death on a former attorney who she said had helped her set up an offshore bank account.

As to explaining Sante's son's testimony she said, "The prosecutors forced her son to testify by threatening him with the Death Penalty." She went on to praise her son and stated that he was a wonderful boy and a hero and she begged the prosecutor to leave him alone. She accused the prosecutor of paying witnesses to lie. Then Sante said to the prosecutor, "You're the real murderer here. You don't know what justice is." The prosecutor could have fired back about all the murders Sante had been involved in. However, Ms. Hunter exercised restraint and didn't call Sante the 'real murderer' since that was the job for the jury to do.

At the time for Rebuttal Testimony the prosecutor recalled Kenny to explain in more detail Sante's role in the killing of banker Syed Ahmed as well as Irene Silverman. This recall was to answer the Defense's claim that Sante wasn't at all involved and knew little or nothing about them. This seemed to end the evidence stage of the trial. However, Sante insisted over her attorney's advice to testify again in surrebuttal.

Sante testified to how wealthy she was at the time of her husband's death. She wanted the jury to know that she was wealthy and had no need to commit crimes for financial gain. It may have seemed like a brag fest in that she had more money than the jurors. Then, after being cross-examined, Sante sat down at counsel table and everyone thought it was over.

Both sides had rested their case and it was time to start the Argument. All of a sudden Sante requested one more time to testify. Everyone wondered what was going on. The judge, not wanting to create an issue on appeal, agreed that she could testify for a third time. Sante walked up to the witness stand and the judge instructed her that she was still under oath to tell the truth.

As she sat in the witness chair, she started spewing out words that seemed more like rambling on and on about Ahmed's murder in that Kenny wasn't in the Grand Caymans at the time of the killing. All she knew was that the banker had disappeared. Regarding the Silverman murder, she testified that she never intended to steal from or kill her since she loved the woman. She explained to the jury that she had no motive to steal from her since she had lots of money. Sante's attorney, who seemed to be shaking his head, asked the judge to erase all of Sante's testimony. This objection surprised the judge since there was no such legal objection. The judge denied the objection and must have pondered, how could this case get any stranger?

Finally, it was time for Argument. Prosecutor Eleanor Hunter was in a league all by herself. She had taken on some of the toughest cases ever handled by the LA DA's Office. She was one of the prosecutors on the Kathleen Soliah case, in which the defendant insisted that she be called Sara Jane Olson in the courtroom. That defendant was one of the Symbionese Liberation Army (SLA) members who planted bombs under LAPD police cars in the 1970s. This fugitive was on the run for 30 years until she was discovered living as a doctor's wife in Wisconsin. This case involved using Patty Hearst as a witness, since she had been kidnapped by the SLA in Berkeley and later joined and lived with the group. That was a tough case that needed a prosecutor who was tough as nails to take the jabs from certain elements who wanted these urban terrorists to be glorified. This prosecutor was well organized since the evidence had to be dug up from old FBI reports. Her perseverance made for an airtight case in which the former SLA member pleaded guilty and served her time in state prison.

The prosecutor, Eleanor Hunter, had been involved in trying the Bruce Koklich case, in which a successful real estate couple's marriage was unraveling. The wife mysteriously disappeared, and her car was later found in a crime-infested area of Long Beach. Her husband continued to hold news conferences in which he pleaded that she be found and returned. With intense investigation, it was determined that the husband had a motive to kill his wife to prevent a costly divorce and to permit him to enjoy the affection of younger companions. The victim's body was never found, and the Defense claimed that if there was No Body there was No Case. This prosecutor investigated every piece of evidence and made a Circumstantial Evidence case against the victim's husband. Although the first trial ended in a hung jury, Ms. Hunter didn't attempt to settle the case but vigorously tried the case a second time. Her perseverance paid off and the husband was found guilty of murder.

Later, prosecutor Hunter handled one of the most horrific cases, which involved two families from India who were in the motel business. Two brothers from one family brutally killed another Indian family who had a motel next to their motel. There was a dispute over the alley that ran behind the motels. The prosecutor, Ms. Hunter, used phone records and security cameras to prove the two brothers set the other family's house on fire. The brothers tied up the other family members and had them burned to death. This prosecutor did a magnificent job of presenting the evidence to the jurors so the jury not only found both of the brothers guilty but imposed the death penalty on both of them.

Eleanor Hunter had a 'No Fear' attitude as to any defendant or defense attorney. She knew how to take whatever evidence the police were able to acquire and she knew how to present it to the juries. Her litigation skills were finely polished with a strong emphasis on using graphics to tell the story.

In this **Sante Kimes case**, she used numerous charts to assist the jurors to understand the facts. She utilized a Timeline chart to show all the key dates that the jurors needed to remember. Her dilemma was that there were 24 crucial dates that the jurors needed to remember. She wanted them all to be on one poster so the jurors could see all the events at one time. However, with 24 lines it made the font so small on the chart that it was difficult for the jurors to read from a distance. The solution was to use two readable charts that could be displayed next to each other.

Prosecutor Hunter used visuals that showed the Relationship of the Parties in the case. Another visual was of the various locations that the jurors needed to be familiar with. One of the most confusing parts of Sante's case was all the documents involving the loan transaction. So the prosecutor labeled them and displayed them on one large visual aid. Ms. Hunter gave an insightful Argument explaining all the pieces of evidence and how they all fit together. She realized that her main job was convincing the jurors that they could believe Kenny Kimes as a witness. She continually used visuals that corroborated every part of his testimony.

She knew that some jurors might look at Kenny as the biggest Judas, since he was selling out his mother in order to save his life. Neither Kenny nor Sante was a likable character, and some would say they were high on the list of being the most despicable human beings on this earth. Ms. Hunter knew that she could only use Kenny's testimony as the basic framework of the case and she needed all those other witnesses to provide the details.

After the prosecution Argument, the Defense attorney commenced his Argument. He did his best to hammer away at Kenny as being unbelievable. He stressed that Sante wasn't anywhere near the killing of David Kazdin in Granada Hills. He harped on the fact that the prosecution hadn't proved their case beyond a reasonable doubt. He reminded the jurors that other people might want the victim killed. Regrettably for her attorney, Sante didn't make a good witness for the Defense. Her continual broad-brush denials made her far from a sympathetic witness. All her attorney could hope for was that some juror might hang up the jury.

After five days of deliberation, the jury had reached a verdict. Sante was brought into the courtroom. She contritely sat down at counsel table and rested her head on her hands with her elbows affixed to the top of the table. She gave the appearance of praying to some God who would be able to save her. Then the jury handed over their verdict to the courtroom clerk who announced in a firm voice – GUILTY OF FIRST DEGREE MURDER.

On March 21, 2005, it was time for sentencing. Sante was fighting to the very end as she told the judge, "We are INNOCENT! I pray for justice. I ask for all Americans to help us. We have only just begun to fight." The judge seemed unmoved by Sante's plea. The judge said, "You are one of the most **EVIL** individuals that I have ever encountered in 16 years on the bench." Thereupon the judge sentenced Sante Kimes to Life Without the Possibility of Parole. Shortly thereafter, Kenny received the same sentence, even though the judge said, "At least he finally stepped up to the plate. I do think it was a real turning point in his life to cut that umbilical cord or whatever, the stranglehold she had on him. I know that his testimony was crucial to her conviction."

On the following graphic page is the summary chart of the Kimeses case which was displayed at the LAPD Homicide Exhibit in Las Vegas.

Graphics 17

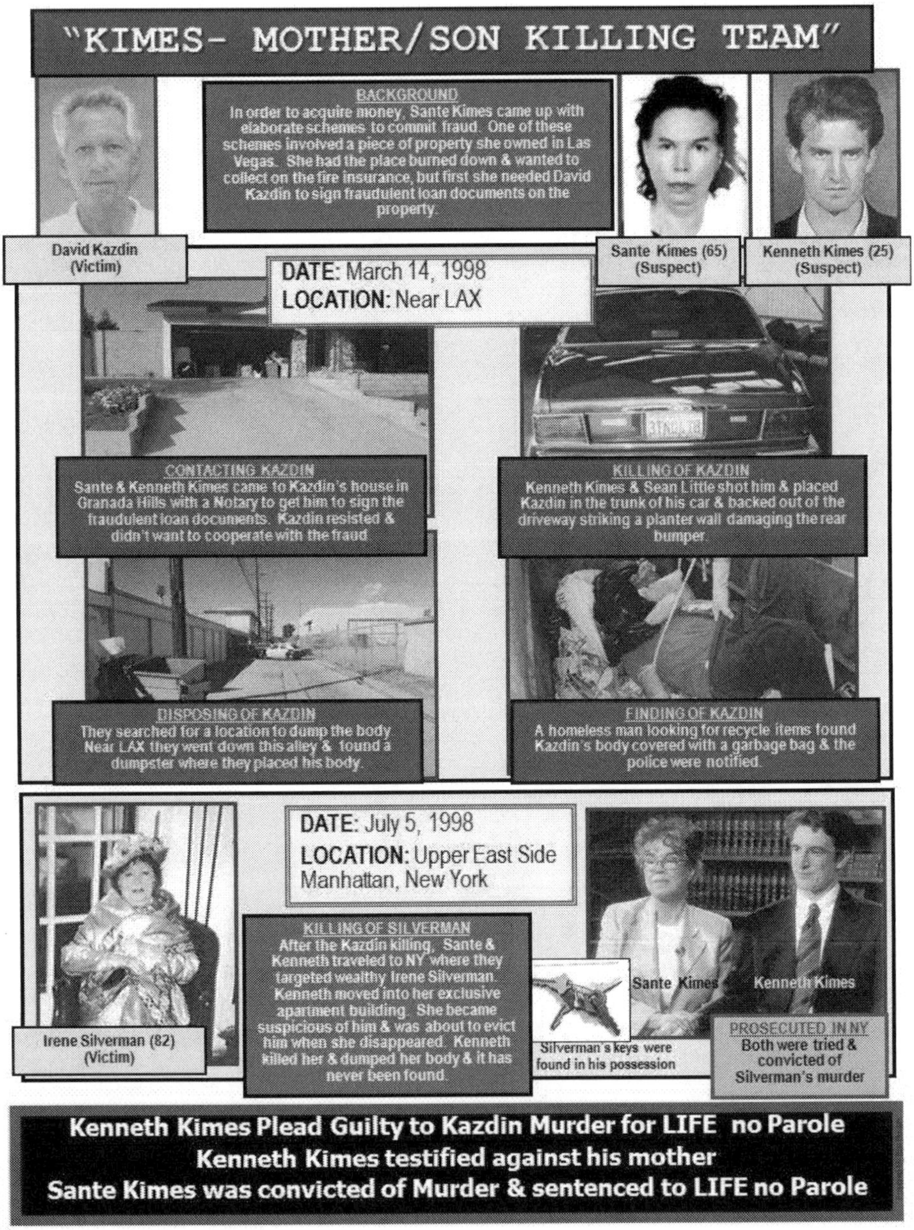
"KIMES- MOTHER/SON KILLING TEAM"
BACKGROUND
In order to acquire money, Sante Kimes came up with elaborate schemes to commit fraud. One of these schemes involved a piece of property she owned in Las Vegas. She had the place burned down & wanted to collect on the fire insurance, but first she needed David Kazdin to sign fraudulent loan documents on the property.
David Kazdin (Victim)
Sante Kimes (65) (Suspect)
Kenneth Kimes (25) (Suspect)
DATE: March 14, 1998
LOCATION: Near LAX
CONTACTING KAZDIN
Sante & Kenneth Kimes came to Kazdin's house in Granada Hills with a Notary to get him to sign the fraudulent loan documents. Kazdin resisted & didn't want to cooperate with the fraud
KILLING OF KAZDIN
Kenneth Kimes & Sean Little shot him & placed Kazdin in the trunk of his car & backed out of the driveway striking a planter wall damaging the rear bumper.
DISPOSING OF KAZDIN
They searched for a location to dump the body Near LAX they went down this alley & found a dumpster where they placed his body.
FINDING OF KAZDIN
A homeless man looking for recycle items found Kazdin's body covered with a garbage bag & the police were notified.
DATE: July 5, 1998
LOCATION: Upper East Side Manhattan, New York
Irene Silverman (82) (Victim)
KILLING OF SILVERMAN
After the Kazdin killing, Sante & Kenneth traveled to NY where they targeted wealthy Irene Silverman. Kenneth moved into her exclusive apartment building. She became suspicious of him & was about to evict him when she disappeared. Kenneth killed her & dumped her body & it has never been found.
Silverman's keys were found in his possession
Sante Kimes
Kenneth Kimes
PROSECUTED IN NY
Both were tried & convicted of Silverman's murder
Kenneth Kimes Plead Guilty to Kazdin Murder for LIFE no Parole
Kenneth Kimes testified against his mother
Sante Kimes was convicted of Murder & sentenced to LIFE no Parole

CHAPTER 46 SIMILARITIES BETWEEN OLD LADIES

What we have learned from these two separate cases is there are a number of similarities between **Helen Golay** and **Sante Kimes**. Olga Rutterschmidt on the other hand grew up in Hungary and was mainly submissive to her crime partner, Helen Golay.

Helen Golay was born in Eastward, Texas, and not far from Oklahoma City, Oklahoma where Sante Kimes was born. Both grew up in a poor dysfunctional family. Strange how both got into crime as teenagers committing shoplifting. They graduated to a higher level of fraud. As young women they were plotters who wanted to outsmart other people. Originally, they didn't want to use violence such as robbery to gain money or property. They perfected their skills by mastering forgery and writing insufficient funds checks.

Much of their theft was by fast talking and hiding the ball. For Helen Golay, she learned from her real estate negotiations that money could be made from dealing with older people who were overly trusting. She found victims who weren't sophisticated at business and she would gain their confidence.

As to Sante, she learned that boldness was disarming. It only took Sante a little fast talking to take the Cadillac from the dealership for a test drive that lasted for more than a month. The taking of the fur coat from the Mayflower Hotel seemed a little audacious, but she had no hesitancy of doing it in front of dozens of people. Later, she used her business acumen to set her houses on fire in order to collect on the fire insurance. Land investment deals had taught her all the procedures and documents needed in real estate transactions.

Sante gained experience as to making money by taking short cuts and being willing to forge a few documents. Her transactions involving the Geronimo Way property were a culmination of all she had learned. She combined her property skills with her insurance fraud skills. Trying to acquire Irene Silverman's property was the ultimate fraud, which included boldness and business smarts. The transition from fraud to murder was easy since she considered it no more than a business decision.

As to both Helen Golay and Sante Kimes, they didn't have any moral problem in eliminating people who stood in the way of completing their fraud. Neither viewed the victims as fellow human beings. Helen Golay thought of the homeless as lesser than human in that they weren't contributing to society but were like parasites living off of others. She used these destitute souls without any human feeling for them. They were mere objects to be used in her elaborate insurance fraud schemes.

As for Sante Kimes, she likewise used the homeless shelters as a recruiting system to supply homeless men whom she would use as pawns in her insidious schemes. Sante had no reservations about traveling to Mexico to entice young women to come with her to the states, where she treated them sadistically and subjected them to abusive conditions using them as human slaves. She preyed on their vulnerability and took advantage of them.

Neither Helen nor Sante needed the money from their scams but had a fatal attraction to making **MONEY** off the backs of the downtrodden. If these women didn't need the money, why would they act in such a diabolical manner? Helen Golay befriended her homeless men and kept them alive for two long years with the knowledge that she would have to kill them. Most people who associate with a group of people for lengthy periods of time somehow develop some type of relationship with those individuals. It is understood that farmers and many 4H members develop a bond with certain animals and agonize over butchering them. But Helen didn't seem to have any attachment to the men she would personally slaughter by driving over them in order to collect on their life insurance.

What was odd about the demise of their victims was that neither Helen nor Sante took any delight in the actual killing of their victims. Many serial killers have a thirst for the actual killing, to the point that too many of them feel a sexual high and enjoy the sense of ultimate control over others. For Helen and Sante it was like a mere business transaction. In order to complete a business deal, one has to do the final act such as handing over the merchandise.

Both women felt they had invested so much of their time and effort in their schemes. Helen had made all the rent payments for the housing of the homeless men. Sante had spent hours of her time perfecting the forgery of all the necessary documents. In a perverse way there was a feeling that they had earned the right to take the life of their victims because of all the time and resources invested in the fraud.

These two murderers set themselves apart from other killers. Some kill because of an argument. Others kill because they have to protect themselves from being caught, such as in a robbery or in a situation when they kill to prevent witnesses from incriminating them. In Helen's and Sante's situations, the killings were business decisions. Helen needed the homeless men dead not because she was mad at them or they could be witnesses but for the mere fact that the insurance companies wouldn't pay unless they were dead. In Sante's case, Irene Silverman had to be killed since she would never have sold her hotel-mansion if she were alive. It had nothing to do with being irate at Irene or her being a witness.

The other thing that was different about these women murderers was the amount of planning involved. Both women were amazingly detailed and prided themselves on their organization skills. They had an uncanny approach that left nothing to chance. Helen's brilliance regarding details made her one of the most gifted murderers of all time. She would never have been caught if she hadn't been so greedy in taking out so many life insurance policies. She wasn't tripped up by lack of planning but only by unrestrained avarice.

Sante pursued Irene Silverman for months, acquiring personal information such as her Social Security number and doing title searches of her property. Sante's planning was meticulous, with the "i's" dotted and the "t's" crossed. Again, she likewise left nothing to chance. We don't know if she would have ever been caught for the fraud/murder scheme against Irene. If the detectives hadn't been looking for them in the defrauding the Utah Car Agency, possibly Sante would have gotten away with Irene's murder. It was all the forged documents that were seized fortuitously in the Lincoln Town Car and Sante's satchel that alerted the police to their involvement in the New York murder.

Paradoxically, both ladies were not caught due to poor planning on their part. Their demise was merely caused by **detective curiosity**. Helen was brought down when two detectives sitting across from each other in the detective bureau started comparing their cases. One detective joked about two old ladies asking for a police report on a hit-and-run accident. The other detective said that was ironic in that he had had a similar case several years earlier. The second detective took the initiative to walk to the Cold Case files and picked up the old case. Then he came back and asked the first detective what were those ladies' names. That was when the names Helen Golay and Olga Rutterschmidt were mentioned and the first detective's eyes lit up and he said those were the same women as in his case.

The same occurred in Sante's case when the detective who was watching TV heard about the Missing Person named Irene Silverman and a person of interest by the name of Manny Guerrero. That detective recognized those names from the seized property when arresting a mother-son team. The fugitive detective contacted the the Missing Person detective and, bingo, the connection was made. Both women had their criminal careers cut short because of **detective curiosity.**

Both women were excellent in covering their tracks. Many murderers are proficient as to the killing part but don't have a so-called "get-away plan." An example of Helen's shrewdness was how careful she was to make sure she had only **one policy from each insurance company for each victim**. This eliminated any insurance company being alerted by the fact they had numerous policies on a victim. The same thing was true with Sante. To illustrate her keen criminal mind, she brought a trusted friend from Las Vegas, Stanley Peters, to come to New York to run the Hotel-Mansion **while she stayed in the background**.

One of the major differences between the women was that Helen had to have the men's bodies found in order to collect on the Accidental Death Insurance. However, in Sante's case the family motto was 'No Body, No Case.' In the killing of David Kazdin, Kenny tried his best to dispose of the body in a trash dumpster. He covered the body with trash bags and placed it deep in the trash dumpster. Unfortunately for Sante and Kenny, there was no way of anticipating that a regular **'dumpster diver'** would be climbing into their particular dumpster. When they killed the banker in the Grand Caymans, his body was well anchored and sank in the ocean and never was found. Earlier in Sante's career, she and her husband worked with an attorney in their arson insurance fraud schemes. When they learned this attorney had become an informant for the FBI, they invited him to join them on a vacation to Costa Rica. They had him killed and his body has never been recovered. Finally, Irene Silverman was Sante's last victim. Sante and Kenny did such an excellent job of disposing of her body that she still has never been found.

The crucial question is what makes a human being like Helen Golay or Sante Kimes into a callous heartless killer. Most likely their chaotic childhood programmed them to have sociopathic characteristics. Both were able to get away with petty larceny without getting caught. On the rare occasions they got caught, they were able to talk their way out of the situation. Helen may have been more successful, or maybe lucky, to weasel her way through various fraudulent real estate deals.

Sante prided herself in having a sixth sense to be able to slither her way out of the grasp of the long arm of the law. However, the turning point of her life was when she went to federal prison for the slavery of the Mexican women. Sante's prison experience indelibly etched in her brain that she would do anything, including killing witnesses, to make sure she never was sent back to the slammer. Most criminologists believe that prison needs to be a negative experience to prevent the person from continuing to commit crime. Unfortunately for the Sante type of criminal, prison doesn't deter them from committing crime but only makes them more desperate to never getting caught.

For all the Helen Golays and the Sante Kimeses in the world, everyone needs to remember the old saying, **“Beware of Wolves in Sheep’s Clothing.”** That saying comes from the Gospel of Matthew 7:15: “Beware of false prophets, which come to you in sheep’s clothing, but inwardly they are ravening wolves.” Those words used 2000 years ago, still apply today in the form of GRANDMOTHERLY types who are MURDERERS.

CHAPTER 47 EPILOGUE

Sante Kimes

On May 19, 2014, she was found dead from natural causes in her cell at Bedford Hills Correctional Facility in New York.

Books written about Sante and Kenny include: *Son Of A Grifter* and *The Mother, The Son, and the Socialite.*

A TV movie, "Like Mother Like Son: The Strange Story of Sante and Kenny Kimes" starring Mary Tyler Moore as Sante Kimes, aired in 2001. Also, Lifetime aired "A Little Thing Called Murder" and featured in one of the episodes of Dateline.

Kenny Kimes

He continues to serve his life sentence in California, not New York, at the Richard J. Donovan Correctional Facility in San Diego.

Kent Walker

Sante's eldest son was 12 years older than Kenny. He wrote a book about his life with his mother, Sante, titled *Son of a Grifter: The Twisted Tale of Sante and Kenny Kimes, The Most Notorious Con Artists in America.* He almost ended up being an accomplice in crime for his mother. He relates when he was 8 years old his mother asked him to go back into the house to retrieve some papers that she had left there. After obediently fetching the papers, he exited the front door as the house exploded in fire. He jumped into the car as his mother accelerated to get away. Sante had no qualms about risking her son's life in order to continue her life of crime.

He gave another example of his mother's love for him. They were in a Palm Springs store when his mother stole a dress and was running out of the store with him. The manager of the dress store chased after them. When she heard sirens approaching, Sante made a fist with her hand and punched her son, Kent, as hard as she could. As a result, his mouth began to bleed. As the police officer arrived, Sante told the officer that the manager had hit her son. The officer placed the store manager under arrest and Sante took Kent to the hospital for stitches to the face. Sante had no shame in using her children for her benefit.

Kent, the oldest son felt, that his younger brother, Kenny, didn't have a chance to escape the grasp of his mother. Kent was glad he was able to distance himself from his mother. He didn't select an exciting life like his brother and had his own vacuum cleaner business in San Diego. Kent is happily married with two children. What a contrast between two brothers, Kent the older, and Kenny the younger.

Eleanor Hunter

She remained with the DA's Office for another year after the Kimes case and she filed her judgeship papers with the Governor's Office. Within a short time, she was appointed as a judge of the Superior Court in Los Angeles County. Most of her tenure as a judge has been in the Compton Courthouse, where she presides over an endless supply of Murder cases.

OTHER BOOKS

By Ronald E Bowers

If you enjoyed this book, take a look at my other books I have written.

My tenth book was titled the *Celebrity Curse.* This book reviewed the mysterious deaths of celebrities starting with the investigation into **Marilyn Monroe's** death. For over a half a century there has been a growing controversy over her untimely death. Was it an accidental overdose or a suicide? However, over the years more facts have revealed the possibility that she may have been murdered. This book considers all the possibilities trying to separate fact from fiction.

Also included in this book is a behind the scenes look at the case of the enablers in the strange death of **Anna Nicole Smith** which resulted in one of the strangest prosecutions of all times. Further on in the ***Celebrity Curse*** we discuss the mysterious deaths of **John Belushi, Natalie Wood** as well as old-time screen legend **Thelma Todd**. Of course the book wouldn't be complete without including the prosecution of **Michael Jackson's** doctor who was giving the superstar an IV drip of Propofol to assist him in sleeping.

Another aspect of the book ***Celebrity Curse*** is a review of a number to Stalking the Stars cases which include **Madonna, Mel Gibson, Catherine Zeta Jones, John Cusack** and **Steven Spielberg**. Here we discuss the high price of being a celebrity with its loss of privacy and threats to one's life and family members. Without a doubt Stalkers are truly a **CELEBRITY CURSE**.

My next book delved into the subject of capital punishment. It was titled the *Death Penalty Designee.* Capital Punishment is considered the third hot button issue after Abortion and Gun Control that most people try to avoid discussing. Everyone has some type of emotional attachment either for or against the Death Penalty without truly understanding the purpose or operation of the Death Penalty. The book doesn't take sides but provides the reader with facts and figures to support their positions. The issues are viewed through the eyes of a person, The Death Penalty Designee, who had to make the ultimate decisions of some of the most notorious cases of all times. The book starts with the Tookie Williams case and continues on with the Richard Ramirez (Night Stalker) case followed by the Bitter and Norris case eventually discussing dozens of homicides that everyone has faded memories of.

Another book was the *Killings on Route 66.* Part of American history can be told by all who have come west on the old Route 66. This book starts at the very end of Route 66 which is the Santa Monic pier where a number of nefarious cases occurred. Next we travel a few blocks to one of the sites where 10 innocent peoples were slaughtered. We follow Route 66 as it traverses through West Hollywood where Dominick Dunn became inspired to be a celebrated True Crime writer. Further on we come across the most horrific and diabolical double murder of all times in Hollywood. Of course we touch upon Dr. Haing Ngor's Killing Fields this time of LA as we stop for a deadly Dodger's game. It's amazing that not all the carnage on Route 66 came from traffic accidents.

A similar book I wrote was the *Killers on Mulholland Drive.* Here I travel down the highway to the Homes of the Stars. I start out relating the sad case of Ennis Cosby who was the victim of a Robbery Gone Bad. Then we weave our way on top of this famous highway to the estate of Marlon Brando where murder raised its ugly head by his son shooting his half-sister's finance while he sat on the sofa watching TV. We can't ignore what happened in his neighbor's house that being Jack

Nicholson. That was where Roman Polanski seduced a 14 year old girl and ultimately he became America's most famous fugitive. We examine how this road is Hollywood's Lovers Lane and at times it leads to deadly consequences.

One of my Celerity books was the *Killing in the Castle.* Most readers are familiar with Phil Spector, the music producer, who brought us the 'Wall of Sound' and who was accused of killing an actress in his castle/house. However, few people know the true story of how this case labeled the 'Battle of the Experts' resulted in a hung jury. This case illustrates what happens when the defendant has unlimited resource and can hire dozens of Defense attorneys to represent him.

This next book was personal in nature for me to write. *Killing of a Legend* involved the double murder case of Mike Thompson the famous auto racing legend and his wife was one of the longest Unsolved Mysteries. A fledgling energetic Sheriff's detective took a new look at this old case and followed up on some obscure facts that unlocked the key to this case. This is a book about two men with giant egos in which one couldn't accept defeat. They took their disagreement all the way to the U.S. Supreme Court.

A slightly different home was the *Rich Kid Killers of Beverly Hills.* This book examines the infamous Billionaire Boys Club killing which was the genesis for the Menendez Brothers massacre of their parents. How could rich kids who have experienced the good life and were well educated turn to murder? Most people think that only the poor or less affluent commit crime. Although rich kids' motives to kill are quite different from the poor or gang shootings, however they do occur and can be difficult to solve.

Another book was the *Killers on the Way to Vegas.* This book tells the story of two mothers who traveled halfway around the world to find their missing sons. It involved a case that fell between the cracks because the mothers didn't know where their sons were when they went missing. This is a story of how strong two mothers' love can be .They wouldn't accept defeat and ended up on the doorstep of the FBI in Los Angeles. There agents stepped up to the plate to solve one of the most mysterious cases by using a cadaver dog to sniff out a grave in the desert on the way to Vegas.

The LA True Crime series all began with this book the ***Killer at the Door.*** It discusses one of those cases in which the DA's Office originally prosecuted the wrong suspect. This book shows how a prosecutor had to right a wrong in order to get the killer at the door. The case has so many twists and turns over a ten year period it took to solve. A long the way this book will introduce the reader to the celebrity world as well as some of the zaniest characters you could ever image.

Made in United States
Orlando, FL
04 November 2026

90205464R00157